OUR STRUGGLE
FOR
INDEPENDENCE

OUR STRUGGLE FOR INDEPENDENCE

Eye-witness accounts from the pages of *An Cosantóir*

EDITED BY
TERENCE O'REILLY

MERCIER PRESS
IRISH PUBLISHER – IRISH STORY

MERCIER PRESS

Cork

www.mercierpress.ie

Trade enquiries to CMD,
55A Spruce Avenue, Stillorgan Industrial Park,
Blackrock, County Dublin

© *An Cosantóir*, 2009

ISBN: 978 1 85635 614 5

10 9 8 7 6 5 4 3 2 1

A CIP record for this title is available from the British Library

Mercier Press receives financial assistance from the Arts
Council/An Chomhairle Ealaíon

Printed and bound in the EU.

CONTENTS

INTRODUCTION

For various reasons, attempts to chronicle the Irish War of Independence (1919–21) did not begin in earnest until the 1950s. The Anvil Press published a series of books including *With the IRA in the Fight for Freedom* and *Dublin's Fighting Story*, all of which carried valuable first-hand accounts of ambushes and actions during this period. Ernie O'Malley gathered many accounts from Old IRA veterans, which originally appeared in a newspaper serialisation and eventually in book form (*Raids and Rallies*) in 1982. O'Malley had already published his own account of the Black and Tan War in 1936; *On Another Man's Wound* was regarded as a work of literary as well as historic merit.

By far, the most comprehensive effort to chronicle the War of Independence was that carried out by the Bureau of Military History. Established in 1947 by Defence Minister and 1916/War of Independence veteran Oscar Traynor, the Bureau employed a staff of civilians and army officers trained in interview skills. In ten years the BMH gathered 1,773 witness statements from participants in the Easter Rising and the War of Independence. Information was given under a guarantee of confidentiality, and the statements were eventually only made public in 2003.

There was however an earlier collection of accounts of this conflict: those published in the Irish military journal *An Cosantóir* between 1940 and 1942.

In June 1940, the armies of Hitler's Third Reich over-ran Western Europe. With the fall of France, Ireland realised that it faced a serious threat of invasion and quickly looked to its defences. Following a joint appeal by all three main political parties the Irish

Defence Forces increased from 21,500 troops (regular and mobilised reservists) in June to 37,000 men by September. Also established was a new reserve force of part time volunteers. The new Local Security Force (LSF) was said to be based on the British Local Defence Volunteers (later renamed the Home Guard), although the Irish version was organised into an A Group and a B Group, the former intended to serve as a military force with the latter (comprising the older volunteers) effectively functioning as an unarmed police reserve.

The new force was originally the responsibility of the Garda Síochána: this was not an ideal situation for the A Group who required military organisation and training. This was eventually provided by the PDF, but in 1940 the army was too heavily committed to its own expansion to be able to provide much assistance. In the early days the LSF had to largely fend for itself.

It was soon apparent that the new force bore many similarities to the Old IRA of 1919. Indeed, many members of the LSF were veterans of the War of Independence, and from an early stage the LSF was demonstrating a certain aptitude for guerrilla type warfare. Most LSF units selected locations suitable for ambushes in their locality while most units included a 'demolition section' which was expected to be proficient with explosives and to be capable of destroying structures such as bridges, many of which were chambered for the purpose.

On 1 January 1941, the LSF A Group was designated the Local Defence Force and came under formal control of the Defence Forces. Colonel M.J. Costello, the O/C Southern Command, had already prepared a training initiative to assist his reservists, namely a weekly military newspaper. Named *An Cosantóir* (*The Defender*) and printed by Paramount Press in Cork, the new publication gave instruction and advice on weapons training, fieldcraft and tactics. In this, Costello was taking a leaf from the Old IRA's book; they had founded their own journal, *An t-Óglach* (*The Volunteer*) as a means of disseminating training material among a widely dispersed part-time force.

Costello had previously been the commandant of the Irish Military College, which he had helped to establish following his graduation from the US army's Command and Staff College, and was able to prevail upon former college instructors to contribute material. Costello was also a veteran of the War of Independence (having served in Tipperary as an intelligence officer) and was able to persuade several other veterans then serving with the regular army and the LDF/LSF to provide accounts of actions they had participated in. Such accounts of guerrilla actions on ground familiar to those reading them were of obvious interest to the LDF who were preparing to fight a similar type of war only twenty years later.

Ironically, at this time the British army, fearing a German invasion and seeking a template for how an island nation might conduct a guerrilla war, were also taking an interest in IRA tactics during the War of Independence. In a memo to the British cabinet in June 1940, General Ismay, a senior British officer on the chief of staff's committee, observed that 'a study of the Irish in the bad times from 1920–1922 should help us here. Our object should be to keep the enemy continually on the jump as we were in Ireland during that period.'

By far the most interesting accounts in this collection are Tom Barry's accounts of the famous ambushes at Kilmichael and Crossbarry, provided under the pseudonym 'Eyewitness'. Probably the most brilliant field commander of the War of Independence, Barry was a die-hard Republican, having taken the anti-Treaty side during the Civil War and remaining active in the government-proscribed IRA until 1938 when he resigned in protest at the decision to commence a bombing campaign in England. He spent the Emergency years acting as an advisor to Colonel Costello's Southern Command.

Another contributor was Seán Gaynor, formerly commandant of the Old IRA Tipperary No. 1 Brigade and in 1941 a district leader with the LDF, who gave his account of the Modreeny Ambush.

Major Joseph V. Lawless, only nineteen when he took part in the action at Ashbourne, was a regular officer commanding the LDF in north Dublin when he wrote his account. Retiring as a Colonel in 1958, he established a tradition of family service in the Defence Forces, his son serving in the Congo in 1960 and subsequently becoming a colonel himself.

A few of the accounts were actually written a short time after the occurrences described. Commandant M. O'Kelly's account of the burning of the Custom House was originally delivered as a lecture to the Infantry School in 1935, while Lieutenant Quirke's account of the operation at Kilmallock was originally published in *An t-Óglach* in 1926.

After the end of the Emergency in 1945, *An Cosantóir* became the journal of the Irish Defence Forces and thrives as such to this day.

THE MEN OF 1916

Pádraig Pearse's tribute to the rank and file:

'I desire now, lest I may not have an opportunity later, to pay homage to the gallantry of the soldiers of Irish freedom who have during the past four days been writing with fire and steel the most glorious chapter in the history of Ireland. Justice can never be done to their heroism, to their discipline, to their fiery and unconquerable spirit, in the midst of peril and death.

'Let me, who have led them into this, speak, in my own and my fellow commanders' names, and in the name of Ireland present and to come their praise, and ask those who come after them to remember them.

'For four days they have fought and toiled, almost without cessation, almost without sleep, and in the intervals of fighting, they have sung songs of the freedom of Ireland. No man has complained, no man has asked "Why"? Each individual has spent himself, happy to pour out his strength for Ireland and for freedom. If they do not win this fight, they will at least have deserved to win it. But win it they will, although they may win it in death. Already they have won a great thing. They have redeemed Dublin from many shames, and made her name splendid among the names of cities.'

A SUCCESSFUL RAID

by Captain M. Donegan

In November 1919, the armament of the 3rd Battalion, 3rd Cork Brigade, could not boast of a single service rifle. A few .38 revolvers there were. Still a rifle battalion without a rifle seemed something of a misnomer. Before the month of November was out, however, ten rifles, as many revolvers, Verey pistols, plenty ammunition and various kinds of equipment were listed in the quartermaster's armament columns.

It happened like this. One of our intelligence personnel reported that a small British war vessel, used for submarine chasing during the war (1914–18) and still in Bantry Bay in 1919, which used normally to anchor well out from the pier whenever she visited our port.

On receipt of this information an idea began to take shape in the minds of the battalion staff; an idea that it would be a great stunt to raid this vessel while berthed at the pier and no procure some much needed rifles.

Intelligence

Our information was pretty good. We knew the approximate time at which the boat used to come alongside and hitch up to the pier. We knew that the officers used usually go ashore while the boat was in port. We knew the hotel they used to frequent. We knew

14

the nature of the 'watch' on the vessel herself – one sailor armed with a revolver. We knew in which portion of the boat the rest of the sailors – about fifteen in all – used to be at night-time. We had a good idea where the arms themselves were stored. In a word we knew all about the little ship from the outside at any rate.

All this information was given us by one of our men who worked in another ship in the bay.

We decided to do the 'job'.

Plans

We made a few plans and scrapped them. The job wouldn't be very simple because there was a military and police patrol in Bantry town itself every night quite close to the pier and any bungling or alarm would mean that all on the pier could be immediately cut off and wiped out or captured.

At length we settled on a plan – four of us – Ralph Keyes, now Lieutenant Keyes, 31st Battalion; Michael O'Callaghan, now Judge Advocate General; Seán Cotter, now Lieutenant, 23rd Battalion, and myself were to go on to the pier, jump on board the vessel, overpower the watch, batten down the rest of the sailors, signal to the rest of our men – six in number – who were to be under cover in the railway off the pier and who were to come immediately aboard to take the stuff.

Next we settled on a house in which to dump the booty and we settled on a way back from the pier to this house. So arrangements were complete.

Our armament for the job consisted of two revolvers, held by the advance party and a sledgehammer (if this be armament) held by the men in reserve on the railway line.

It was not, however, a question of arms so much; we had no chance if it came to a show down. It was a question of putting our plans neatly into practice without a shot being fired and our most important ally in achieving this would be, and was, surprise.

The appointed night arrived and at about 8.30 we moved towards the pier as already arranged – in one and twos. We four of the advance party moved in twos as if for a stroll on to the pier. We could hear the sailors singing in the abaft cabin. It was a moonlit night so we could see the sailor on watch standing near the wheel house amidship. He was our immediate objective and we had plans arranged to silence him.

Fortunately we had no occasion to put the plans into operation, because much to our amazement he moved abaft towards the cabin in which the other sailors were singing and descended the ladder, disappearing in front of our eyes, and joining the others below. What prompted him to do this is very hard to say. He may have been going to relieve nature or maybe providence took a hand in the game and urged him to move. Anyway, his head had hardly disappeared below the deck when two of us who had the revolvers jumped on board, ran to the abaft cabin, stuck our revolvers down and ordered all below to remain as they were. The surprise was complete.

I can feel the silence that followed our command even now. We told them that if they remained quiet nothing would happen to them, but that at the slightest movement a bomb would be dropped amongst them. We had of course no bomb to drop and even if we had the dropping of it, it would mean our own undoing, as the military patrol would be on the scene immediately. 'Twas pure bluff, but the bluff worked and worked well. Nobody moved.

While this was happening the other two had jumped aboard the boat, had signalled to the men in reserve on the railway and these now swarmed on deck.

Two men were placed on guard over the sailors in the cabin, and I went forward just in time to see the armoury door being smashed in by a blow from the sledgehammer. I shall never forget the thrill I got on seeing a number of rifles in a rack under the ray of the flashlamp. How regular and uniform rifles look in the rack. That was how they struck me just then. And they were ours for the taking!

And take them we did, eager hands grasped them – ten in all – others stuffed revolvers into their pockets, and all filled ammunition, equipment, etc., into bags which had been brought for the purpose. We cleared out the little room in no time. I gave a full warning to the sailors to stay put for at least half an hour (they didn't obey this order in full; after a quarter of an hour one put his head out the port hole and began to yell and about shout for help) and we all cleared with our booty from the scene.

So far so good: but our job was not yet done. We partly guessed that the sailors would raise the alarm before the half-hour was up and it would not be a difficult job to intercept us getting back. We skirted the town and arrived at a house not one hundred and fifty yards from the military barracks. We then heard the bugles blowing the 'Alarm', and soon lorries began to rush past the house on the road outside, while we disposed safely of our capture inside.

The town was surrounded. Widespread searches were made but no military mind thought of searching a place so near the military post. No trace was found and nobody was arrested.

The struggle for independence in that area now entered upon a new phase. The period of raiding of mails, raiding of houses for arms, etc. had passed: with ten Canadian Ross rifles and plenty of ammunition, bigger game was now hunted: the attacks on barracks and ambush phase was about to begin.

One mistake we made, however; a three inch gun mounted on the bow deck we could, I think, have brought with us. The moral effect of having it would have cleared every police outpost in West Cork but the step from no rifle to a three inch gun was too great even to contemplate. *I ndiaidh a chéile deintear na caisleáin.*

CROSSBARRY

by 'Eyewitness'

This is not the story of the fight between the 3rd (West) Cork Brigade flying column and the British forces at Crossbarry. It is a study of the strategic and tactical factors of the biggest and most successful battle waged against the British during the Anglo-Irish War. It is written as a military article for a military paper in the hope that it may be of use to those who are now studying and training to meet the grim reality of modern invasion. Nor should this article be interpreted as one wherein it is assumed that the Volunteers who fought at Crossbarry and other battles for Irish independence will be absent if attack should again come. On the contrary, there can be no doubt whatever but that the Volunteers of twenty years ago will be found side-by-side in arms with the younger men. The only exceptions will be those who are no longer fit to do so.

It need hardly be said that there is a vast difference between the military problems of the fight at Crossbarry nearly twenty years ago and those of a present day defence against invasion. Then the IRA were badly armed, half-trained bands of volunteers without co-ordinating organisation attempting to drive out an invader who had been entrenched here for seven hundred years. They numbered at most at any given time about 2,000 armed men. Now there is an organised army of greatly superior numbers who have had the splendid opportunity of training and organising in peace time. There is no need to stress the difference in armament. Despite all this difference certain principles remain paramount in all wars. Leadership, morale, courage, common sense and the efficient movement and disposition of troops before and in battle are as essential to day as they were twenty, a hundred or five hundred years ago if victory is to be won. And make no mistake about it: the army which is higher in these virtues can win against one which has not got them to the same degree even though it should be much larger and far more heavily armed.

The study of the fight at Crossbarry will be more clearly understood when it is taken in sequence under the following headings: (a) The General Situation, (b) Terrain, (c) Enemy Dispositions, (d) Column Dispositions, (e) The Action, (f) The Retirement, (g) The Conclusions.

The General Situation

In March 1921, the Anglo-Irish War had been greatly intensified in about five areas, including West Cork. Although national resistance against British rule and administration was general, real military effort was unfortunately confined to those few areas whose Volunteers hit out, took hammerings and again hit back. Each Brigade was then independent and quite naturally GHQ was in no position to control the fighting in the different brigade areas. There was no co-ordination of activities as each unit fought its own battle, won its own victories or stood up to its own defeats. The morale of civilian population was high, very high in fighting areas, but they had to suffer a ceaseless harassing from the British forces. Faced with this limitation of real military effort to a few areas only, the British High Command quite logically concentrated on wiping out the fighting men of the active districts.

The West Cork Brigade was then composed of about 3,000 active Volunteers, divided into seven battalions of unequal strength. Twenty-six officers and men had been killed in action, a good number wounded, and many hundreds were in jails.

The brigade armament was one hundred rifles, thirty-seven rounds per rifle, sixty revolvers with very little ammunition, about seventy shot-guns, some explosives and about a dozen 'Mills' bombs. Practically the whole of this was captured from the British in fights or in raids.

About the middle of 1920 a small flying column was formed for attacks on the enemy, but as arms continued to be captured in these attacks and the enemy as a result operated in stronger forces, it was both possible and imperative to increase the strength of the West Cork Brigade column. In mid-March 1921 it numbered one hundred and three officers and men who were selected for their efficiency, courage and endurance. Most of them knew their fate, if captured, would be execution under the martial law which then prevailed or more likely before they reached a jail or barracks. The column was armed with all the armament of the brigade except the shot-guns. It was organised into seven sections each having a section commander and thirteen men. It was officered by a commanding officer, adjutant, quartermaster and medical officer. Intelligence was supplied by the brigade IO and the battalion intelligence officers through whose area the column operated. There was a column piper.

The enemy strength was difficult to compute, mainly because the British troops from the adjoining IRA brigade area, garrisoned at Cork city, Ballincollig, Macroom and Kinsale operated extensively in West Cork. Bandon, Clonakilty, Skibbereen, Dunmanway, Bantry and Bere Island were all strong enemy garrisons in addition to which there were numerous Black and Tan posts. A fair estimate of the number of enemy forces available for immediate action against the West Cork IRA, was 12,000 of all arms. By March 1921, they operated mainly on foot in columns of two hundred, generally two or more columns travelling through the country on parallel lines a few miles apart.

Information was received that about three hundred soldiers of the Essex regiment were to move by road from Kinsale to Bandon on St Patrick's Day, 1921. The brigade column took positions before dawn on that day to attack them at Shippool, which is about half-way between Kinsale and Bandon. The enemy moved out from Kinsale, but were stopped en route and told that the column was waiting for them. They returned to Kinsale. The column commander received this information at 4.30 p.m. and immediately ordered the retirement of the column from the ambush position to Skeugh which is east of Innishannon. There it was billeted and throughout the following day it waited, receiving some intelligence reports of enemy activities. That night at 10 p.m. it moved off north–north-west to the Crossbarry area where it billeted at about ten houses in the townland of Ballyhandle. By this time it was expected that, following the return to Kinsale barracks of the British, an extensive attack would be made on the column.

Terrain

Crossbarry is situated twelve miles south-west of Cork city. It is about nine miles from Ballincollig, eighteen from Macroom,

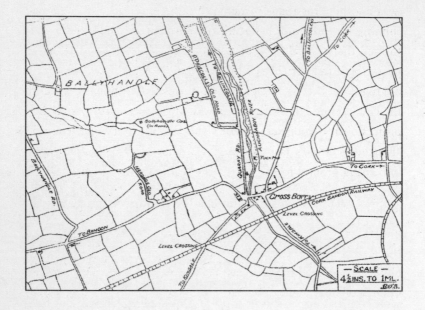

twelve from Kinsale and eight miles from Bandon. The old road from Bandon to Cork, which was and is quite a good road, passes by Crossbarry. Here it is met by two roads from the north and two roads from the south and they form a double crossroads only thirty yards apart. The road from the north running into the western one of those two crossroads flanks that part of Crossbarry and Ballyhandle on its eastern side, where the column was billeted and where the ensuing main action took place. It is known locally as 'The Quarry Road' and by its side down to Crossbarry bridge runs the Aughnaboy river, which can be forded. Three hundred yards north of this road from the Cross is the entrance to O'Driscoll's farmhouse and one hundred and fifty yards west of the house is an old ruin standing in one of O'Driscoll's fields, known as 'The Castlefield'. From the crossroads, travelling westwards, there are two bends and then a straight of two hundred yards. On the roadside and close together are two farmer houses, the eastern occupied by Beasleys and the other by Harolds (then). About half a mile further west another crossroads is met and as the local name for the road running north from it is not for the moment available, and as it is formed the western flank of the action, it shall be known for the purposes of this article as 'The Ballyhandle Road'. Two important old roads or boreens, apart from entrances to farmhouses, ran in to the countryside northwards and both afforded excellent cover and protection for troop movements. The first is an old road running alongside Harold's farmhouse. It winds its way for nearly a mile into rising ground to the north. The second is the old road which forms the entrance to O'Driscoll's farmhouse and which branches off before the road is reached and runs north through Ballyhandle until it comes out at another road connecting the Quarry Road and that called herein 'The Ballyhandle Road'. The countryside north of Crossbarry road rises for several miles except in the area between O'Driscoll's farm and Crossbarry Cross wherein lies a valley which runs north-west for about six hundred yards. The fields are well fenced with strong banks and of average size, well suited to troop movements.

South of the Crossbarry road the ground is low lying and level to a depth of about a mile and a half where the main Cork-Bandon road is reached. Through this country, a few hundred yards south of and parallel to the road, runs the Cork-Bandon railway line. One mile to the east of Crossbarry the Kinsale branch railway line meets this main line at Kinsale Junction. In a little over a mile of the railway line in front of Crossbarry, there are five roads crossing it, connecting the main Cork-Bandon road to the Crossbarry road. There was not a single road cut within miles of this area.

Enemy Dispositions

The West Cork Brigade column was only an hour in billets around Crossbarry when at 2.30 a.m. scouts reported seeing the lights and hearing the noises of lorries about three miles to the west. Ten minutes later a similar report was received of enemy movements to the east. By then there was no doubt that an extensive attack on the column had started. It was not until later, of course, that the following details were confirmed:

At 1 a.m. on the morning of 19 March, four hundred troops left Cork, two hundred Ballincollig, three hundred Kinsale and three hundred and fifty Bandon. Later one hundred and twenty Auxiliaries left Macroom. Still later troops left Clonakilty and more left Cork. They proceeded by lorries to four points, approximately four miles north–north-east, south–south-east and west of Crossbarry. There they dismounted and formed up in columns. About half of each column then moved on foot raiding the countryside as they converged on Crossbarry. The remainder again mounted the lorries and were moved slowly onwards after the raiding columns. Their tactics were apparently those of motorised infantry who could be rushed to any point where the IRA were contacted. This arrangement also allowed of the changing over of raiding troops on foot for the fresh men on the lorries.

They raided and closely searched every house and outhouse in the countryside. Each column took many civilians and some unarmed Volunteer prisoners. One of the eastern columns came to the house three miles north of Crossbarry where Brigade Commandant Charles Hurley was recuperating from a bullet wound. They killed him, but before he died fighting, attempting to breakthrough, he killed one and wounded three of them. Two scouts had been sent on early to bring Charlie Hurley down to the column but had been intercepted on the way and had been taken prisoners. The column clearly heard the shots that killed him at about 6.30 a.m. Thus the British forces made very slow progress as they moved on to where the column was waiting.

Column Dispositions

When the column mobilised at 2.30 a.m. it had full knowledge of the fact that the enemy was moving to attack it from several sides. Although the numbers of the enemy were not then known, the IRA had no doubt that they were outnumbered by ten to one at least. The column commander had to decide without delay whether to fight or to retire and attempt to evade action. The decision to fight was made immediately. Each and all of the following factors governed the decision:

(a) It was extremely doubtful if the IRA column could retire in any direction without being met by superior forces. The only direction from which the British were not known to be advancing was north to north-west. But there was no guarantee that they were not coming that way also. Had the column retired that way and met an enemy force they would have been in a serious position. The enemy would have held the high ground and their tactics need only have been to man the ditches in a 'holding' operation, while the other British columns closed in on the IRA

(b) The IRA column had only thirty-seven rounds per rifle. This shortage demanded initially a swift and intensive fight at close quarters, which if not in itself decisive, would have the effect of upsetting the carefully planned enemy deployment. If the column retired this objective could not have been achieved and the best the column could hope for would be an all-day series of skirmishes with the British who undoubtedly would harass it continuously, even if they did not corner it. The IRA ammunition would not last several hours of this warfare, much less a full day.

(c) A heavy and successful attack on those largescale British rounds-up was an overdue strategic necessity. Hitherto they had not been attacked and there was a grave danger that by their wholesale arrests of Volunteers, captures of dumped arms and intimidation of the civilian population, they would seriously interfere with the Volunteer organisation and damage the morale of the people.

(d) From observations of enemy movements it was clear that the British force from the west would reach Crossbarry sometime before the other British columns. That would even up the opening fight and the column was supremely confident of being able to defeat it and thus smash one side of the encircling wall of troops. This would leave the IRA column free to pass on to the west where it could, according to circumstances, turn either north or south with the practical certainty of avoiding for that day further contact with the British. In addition there was expectation of the column increasing its armament, particularly its ammunition, from such an attack.

The column moved south to Crossbarry about 3.30 p.m. Nos 1, 2, 3, 6 and 4 sections were placed in positions inside the northern ditch of the Crossbarry road and in the houses and outhouses alongside it. The line stretched from where No. 1 section was in position at 'Harold's Old Road' to the bend near Crossbarry crossroads occupied by No. 4. Both those end sections could enfilade the road approaches to their respective positions in addition to their frontal fire. No. 5 section was posted in and in the vicinity of 'The Castlefield' six hundred yards directly in rear of No. 4. They were in a position to cover the left flank and left rear approaches. No. 7 section was placed about six hundred yards to the west of No. 1. From a point about two hundred yards north of the Ballyhandle crossroads they extended northwards, covering the right flank. Nearly half the section were able to fire directly on to the Crossbarry road at and around 'The Ballyhandle Cross'. Three men were detached from Nos 2, 3 and 6 sections and instructed to move directly back behind the attacking positions for over half a mile to patrol east to west behind the column positions. Even though this small group was not strong enough to stop an enemy force moving on the column from the centre rear, they would delay them and give the column time to change deployment. A stone barricade was erected around the bend near Crossbarry Cross and forty and one hundred and forty yards west of it, two powerful observation mines were laid. The piper was placed in the middle of the attacking sections with instructions to play Irish war songs as soon as the fight started. Thus seventy-two officers and men were deployed for attack and thirty one others were protecting their flanks and rear. It was not possible to surprise the column.

The column then received through the section commanders the following action orders:

(a) No section was to retire from its positions without orders, no matter how great the pressure. Arrangement for rapid reinforcement of any point had been made. Even though sections saw no enemy they were not to move to the aid of other sections, as the enemy were operating on various sides.

(b) No Volunteer was in any circumstances to show himself until the action started, for the plan entailed allowing the British forces to move right through the ambush position until the leaders were over the eastern mine when it was to be set off. The order was then to attack the nearest enemy whilst the second mine was to be set off if the enemy came to it.

(c) Communication between the column commander and the various sections were to be made by runners. The command post was movable between Nos 2, 3, and 6 sections.

(d) The direction of retirement would not be given until the move off, but whatever sections were engaged on advance, rear and flank guards, were to keep moving in extended order not nearer than three hundred yards to the main column.

The Action

About 8.15 a.m. a long line of lorries carrying troops travelled very slowly in to the Crossbarry position. There were twelve altogether between Nos 3 and 7 sections but many more stretched back west along the road. Unfortunately a Volunteer, despite the most strict orders, showed himself at a raised barn door and was seen by many of the British. The leading lorry stopped instantly in front of No. 3 section. Some of the soldiers shouted and attempted to jump out, but the order was given to fire, and No. 3 section opened up at it. Immediately Nos 1 and 2 also fired at the lorries immediately in front of them. No. 7 opened fire six hundred yards west at more of the lorries in the vicinity of the Ballyhandle crossroads. Volley after volley was poured in to the British at five or seven yards range and they broke and scattered, leaving their dead, a fair amount of arms and their lorries behind them. The survivors scrambled over the southern ditch and made for the south. Nos 1, 2 and 3 sections were ordered out into the road, and from the southern ditch kept up a rapid fire on the retreating British who had to run through fields which were exceptionally large for that district. The British had very little cover and lost many men. They never stopped retiring until they reached the main Bandon-Cork road, a mile and a half away. Even then they did not attempt to reform but struggled back in groups to Bandon nearly seven miles away. The piper continued to play Irish war tunes. The Volunteers were then ordered to collect the enemy guns and munitions, and amongst the first lot brought in was a new Lewis gun and eight loaded pans which the British got no opportunity to use. The order was then given to start burning the lorries. Nos 4, 5 and 6 sections were not up to then engaged, nor had the patrol in the rear sighted any enemy. As the first three lorries were set on fire, shooting was heard on the eastern flank, and the sections on the road were ordered back to their original action stations. One British column of about two hundred men advanced across the railway line from the south-east. They were attacked by Nos 4 and 6 sections and retired, after heavy fighting. Nor did they renew the attack. They lost several killed. A few minutes afterwards a small contingent of the main western column which had already been smashed up at Crossbarry appeared on the right flank. They were attacked by No. 7 section. This party was apparently left behind the main British column to complete some raids and were on foot. As they advanced they were surprised by several volleys from No. 7 section, and they too retired quickly and were not later seen.

As the fighting at this short encounter died down, fighting started in still another quarter. Back at 'The Castlefield' on the left rear still another British column appeared. They had entered 'Driscoll's Old Road' at its northern end from the road connecting 'The Quarry Road' and the Ballyhandle road. They were unobserved as they travelled south to Driscoll's farmyard, keeping to the side of the old road all the way. They numbered two hundred. This manoeuvre did not, as they hoped, bring them directly to the rear of the column, as O'Driscoll's farmhouse was east of where No. 5 section was posted to cover the left flank of the IRA column. The British column then attempted to move west and south from the farmyard, but were met by rifle fire from No. 5 section. They retired to the farmyard, and whilst some of them kept up a very heavy fire on No. 5 section position, the others attempted an encircling movement by retiring back up 'O'Driscoll's Old Road' and working west of No. 5. By this time two officers and ten volunteers who had been ordered up to reinforce No. 5 arrived. There were now twenty-six volunteers facing the east and their line was extended northwards to counter the anticipated enemy encircling movement. Therefore, when the

British encircling party turned west from O'Driscoll's Old Road twelve volunteers were again waiting for them. The British officer and advanced sections were allowed to come within thirty yards of the waiting volunteers before fire was opened on them. They lost seven dead and retired down 'The Quarry Road.'

No enemy were now in sight in any direction Nos 1, 2, 3, 4 and 6 sections were moved back up 'Harold's Old Road' to a point where No. 5 section was directly east of it and No. 7 section directly west. Both sections were then retired to the main column. Just as the whole column was about to move off remnants of the eastern British columns were seen to be mobilising in a field about nine hundred yards away on rising ground to the east of 'The Quarry Road'. The whole column was deployed along a ditch, the target pointed out, and the range given. Ninety-seven rifles fired round after round into them at nine hundred yards. They broke up and scattered out of sight, and nothing further was seen of any of those columns, although there were two minor engagements in the course of the column retirement, several miles away with fresh British troops.

The column casualties were three volunteers killed and two wounded. The British admitted thirty-nine killed, including five officers, and forty-seven wounded. The column had good reason to believe that the British losses were much greater.

CROSSBARRY II

by 'Eyewitness'

The Retirement

The West Cork Brigade flying column retired to Gurranereagh, which is fourteen miles due west of Crossbarry. Before reaching its destination it had however to travel about twenty miles, as it first moved north–north-west, through Crossbound on to Raheen, where it turned west through Crowhill on to Rearour. For about five miles it marched west–south-west, then turning due west it continued on to cross the Bantry-Crookstown road near Béal na Blath and on to Gurranereagh. The first minor engagement with the enemy on the retirement took place at Crowhill. The right flanking section fired on a body of Auxiliaries, who returned the fire, but who, strangely enough, did not follow up the flankers. There were no IRA casualties, and the Auxiliaries were stated to have had four men hit. Here it should be said that this body of Auxiliaries, numbering one hundred and twenty, were to have participated in the actual round-up at Crossbarry, but through a mistake in the order they went to Kilbarry, which is eight miles away from Crossbarry. Finding none of their comrades there, they returned to Macroom, and were then ordered out for the right destination. The probable reason they did not engage the flankers was they were obeying orders to get to Crossbarry without delay.

A few miles west of Crowhill at Rearour the same column flanking section were fired on by another fresh party of British soldiers. They were fired at from long range and suffered no casualties although two goats grazing near them were killed by the enemy fire. The flanking section did not return the fire but slipped on. Here again there was no attempt made to follow up the column. Perhaps the explanation is that the enemy was only a small party with definite instructions to hold a certain line of country.

It was now nearly 4 p.m. The column had long since placed the wounded in a place of safety, but it was still carrying the captured armaments. The main object of the commander was now to avoid contact until the men were rested and fed. Each hour brought night and darkness nearer and made easier this objective. The column had marched nearly the whole way through fields, boreens and had touched roads only to cross them. The column reached its billets at Gurranereagh without further incident.

Probable Queries

Some probable queries should be anticipated before the lessons of 'Crossbarry' are summarised.

It is not proposed to examine in detail the advisability of operating a unit of over one hundred officers and men such as the West Cork column was with very limited armament and without supporting forces. Many theories can be advanced against it but two facts in support, so far outweigh the theories that they need only be stated. The first fact is that the brigade had no more arms. If it had, there would have been several other columns of equal strength operating in conjunction with and under the brigade column leadership. The second fact is that the brigade column could not have been divided into two or more smaller columns during that period without impairing dangerously its defensive and offensive capabilities. Owing to enemy tactics of operating and travelling in very strong forces, a smaller striking unit of the IRA would have been useless except as a sniping force. Nor could a smaller force successfully defend itself against the largescale rounds up. Therefore the unit had to operate in full strength or not at all and the strategy then was attack and again attack.

The organisation of the column into sections as large as fourteen as against the usual army sections of seven or ten, may also be questioned. Here again it must be clearly remembered that the column was unsupported and had to make its own provisions day and night, on the march and at rest for its own protection. Under those circumstances a small section would not be adequate to stem a flank or rear attack, and the column could not afford to divert two sections to the right, left or rear, when in attack. In addition the advantage of having only one section commander responsible for flank or rear protection is obvious. Each section commander was efficient. Generally speaking the organisation in seven large sections, as against ten smaller ones, was formulated to meet the special conditions then prevailing in West Cork.

The reason may also be asked as to why the column did not cut some of the roads in the vicinity for protection. The column could not even consider the most suitable roads owing to the fact that it was precluded by the enemy's near approach from several directions. If road-cutters had by some chance escaped having been either seen or heard at work, the road cut itself would have quickly told the enemy that the column was near. That would have been fatal to the column's tactics of surprise attack.

Lessons

The following is a brief summary of the lessons which may be learned from Crossbarry:

1. The British failed to complete the encirclement of the column. They should certainly have sent one of the eastern columns to close in from the north–north-west. It may be, of course, that the one hundred and twenty Auxiliaries who came on late owing to a mistake in orders were destined to move on the column from the north–north-west.

2. The British column commander who led his column down 'O'Driscoll's Old Road' to O'Driscoll's farmhouse made a very bad mistake in not leaving the 'Old Road' at least half a mile back to extend westwards. This would have brought him to the rear of the IRA. This officer must have heard the battle going on down the road long before he reached O'Driscoll's farmhouse. Also had he consulted his map he would have seen that the Old Road which he was travelling ran nearly parallel to 'The Quarry Road' and would not bring him out in the rear of the IRA. The only excuse that might be put forward for this officer is that his forces may have observed the patrol of three IRA men guarding the immediate rear, mistaken them for a larger force and wrongly assumed there was a much larger IRA rearguard. The British officer may then have decided to get closer to the column before cutting across its rear and engaging it.

3. Communications between British columns were not good.

4. The British rounding up movements should have been started by daylight. Their closing in tactics were followed by the IRA throughout darkness by lights, noises and the barking of dogs. Those warning of approach would not be given during daylight.

5. The British handling of motorised infantry was defective and slipshod, particularly by the commander of the forces from Bandon. This officer sent at least sixteen lorries of

troops towards or in to the ambush area before a single foot soldier reached it. Probably Crossbarry was the arranged meeting place of the western, eastern and southern British columns, and possibly the commander of the Bandon troops assumed that the other British contingents had already reached there before he ordered his motorised troops on. Whatever the reason the British paid dearly for it.

6. The IRA adopted the only really sound policy left to it by deciding to attack one side of the encircling troops, before the other British forces closed in.

7. The deployment of the IRA main body along the ditch of the road, so as to attack at point blank range ensured a decision in the shortest possible time. And time was the important factor in view of the enemy's probable intention. Despite a natural inclination to use more forces to protect flank and rear approaches the main attacking body of the West Cork column was maintained at an effective strength, even in face of encirclement.

8. The disobeying of the order that no man was to show himself under any circumstances until the fight started endangered not alone the success of the attack, but the safety of the whole column. Had this man been in No. 7 section and in enemy view in that position, the result would have been extremely serious. Luckily the enemy were well into the ambush area before he was observed. Thus, might one man, by disobeying an order, endanger a whole unit's existence.

9. The need of flanking sections as well as advance and rear guards was proved very decisively in the retirement. The IRA column was in danger of ambush throughout the

twenty miles march to billets and strict march discipline had to be maintained right into Gurranereagh.

10. Finally only a unit with very high morale would have passed the test of Crossbarry. This morale arose from each volunteer's belief in the justice of his fight; from his very high discipline, largely self-imposed; from his belief that the supreme attempt at the suppression of his nation had arrived and from the mutual confidence and trust, which existed between officers and men.

Some Comments on Crossbarry
by Colonel M.J. Costello

How is it that this small force greatly out-numbered, vastly inferior in armament and almost completely surrounded, won a clear victory and successfully retired with slight losses? In the answer to this question, is contained the lessons which Crossbarry has for us today.

Leadership

The leadership of Barry's column is obviously the factor of first importance because the matters mentioned in succeeding paragraphs depend upon good leadership. Even a slight acquaintance with war will show clearly that good leadership is essential to success.

Napoleon has put into pithy phrases most of the conclusions to which a study of war will lead us. We will not, however, understand his sayings fully unless we associate them with historical examples, which illustrate them. 'In war,' he says, 'it is not men who count, it is the man.' If the men of Crossbarry had not been led with skill and determination, there would have been no fight to write about. They would simply have been mopped up.

Morale and Discipline

Napoleon also tells us that 'the moral is to the physical as three is to one'. In the superior moral qualities of Barry's column is to be found another reason for the result of the action and an object lesson in the truth and importance of Napoleon's remark. Only men of the very best quality as soldiers would have shown the determination, the calmness and the disregard of odds which were essential to victory. Confidence in their commander and in their other leaders, a confidence learned in other fights, and an intense patriotism were the foundations of this high morale and discipline.

Surprise

Surprise is the greatest weapon in war. It is one of the principles of war, which we deduce from the experience of all history. The value of surprise is well illustrated here. Although the British columns were converging upon the IRA column and presumably searching for it, the IRA column was so skilfully handled and so well concealed that it succeeded in surprising its enemies. The effect of that surprise is clearly seen in the account of the fight.

Security and Thoroughness

In every fight many things are inevitably decided by chance, but the aim of every soldier should be to leave nothing to chance which can be foreseen and provided for in advance. This applies especially to security measures. Whilst we must endeavour to surprise our enemy, we must neglect no means of guarding ourselves against surprise. The security measures at Crossbarry worked. Everything that could be done was done to dispose the column in such a manner that it could meet attack from any direction. Steps were also taken to secure early in formation of the movements and dispositions of the enemy. It is worth the while of every reader to consider what would have been the effect of slipshod methods in this matter; what would have happened if even one step had been neglected, if the leader had been content, as so many of us are prone to be, with something less than absolute thoroughness and attention to every detail in providing for the security of his command.

AN ARMED
NATION

'To carry arms is the first right of man, for arms are the guardians of property, honour, and life. God gave weapons, as well as clothing, to the lion and the eagle; but to man he gave skill to furnish himself with all bodily comforts, and with weapons to defend them, and all his other rights, against every assailant, be he the beast of the forest or the tyrant of society.

'To carry arms is the ultimate guarantee of life, property, and freedom. To be without the power of resisting oppression is to be a slave. What matter that, with delusive words, your rulers says he will not rifle your altars, nor pollute your hearths – what matter that your gaoler boasts his power to protect you, and flourishes his weapon before your cell. Arms and liberty are synonymous. If you see an unarmed and an armed man together, you instantly conclude that the one is a prisoner – the other a guard. Arms are the badges of freemen. He who is unarmed will soon be in chains.'

Thomas Davis

THE AMBUSH AT BALLYVOURNEY

by Mr C. Browne

On Friday, 25 February 1921, took place what has variously been called the Ballyvourney, the Coolavokig, or the Poulnabro Ambush. It was carried out by a flying column of Cork No. 1 Brigade in charge of the O/C 1st battalion acting under the brigade O/C, also present.

Objective

The aim of the attacking party was to surprise and overwhelm an enemy convoy of lorries, secure their much wanted arms and more vital still their stores of ammunition. The IRA supplies of arms and ammunition were obtained almost solely by this method and the success of an engagement was often measured by the amount of such material captured from the enemy.

If we accept this standard alone the ambush could not be called a success as neither arms or ammunition were captured but then it would obviously be wrong when fighting a powerful enemy to overlook the effect on his morale (else the Custom House fight would have been reckoned a failure) and the infliction of heavy casualties. With the latter taken into account the ambush can be termed a definite success.

Number of Men Engaged coming east or west

The attacking party consisted of fourteen rifles and two Lewis Guns from the 1st and 2nd battalions, twenty-three rifles and four shot-guns from the 7th Battalion, and twenty-three rifles and twenty-six shot-guns from the 8th Battalion. It had no grenades or other equipment. The enemy force originally engaged comprised one hundred and twelve Auxiliaries travelling in nine lorries and one car, and it was well armed with rifles, machine guns and grenades. After a lapse of three hours this was supplemented by some hundreds of military equipped with armoured cars and an aeroplane.

The Position

The position on the main Macroom-Killarney road about seven miles from Macroom and two miles from the village of Ballymakera, offered distinct advantages for surprise and attack and in its ruggedness afforded excellent means for retreat. As seen on the attached sketch (see page 42) it was on a winding road flanked on the north side by continuous rocky ground varying ten to fifteen feet in height. On the southern side were some isolated rocks from which, owing to the sunken ground between them and the road, there was an excellent field of fire.

The position was marred somewhat by the two cottages at the south side of the road at the eastern end. The western one of these was dominated by the positions immediately across the road from it and it was felt that it would be dangerous because of possible cross-fire to occupy it as a post. The eastern cottage with a blind gable facing the road and having no command of it was useless as a post. Both however should have been barricaded to prevent enemy occupation.

Disposition of Column

The column first moved into position at daybreak on 18 February. The forward Lewis gun was placed at the point marked A on the map and had a fine field of fire in front to the cottage along the road to the north-east as far as the cross, and along the road to the south as far as the bend. No. 1 section was in position around this point covering a like area of road. It also covered a permanent block on the minor road, this being out of sight of the main road and arranged to prevent lorries from forcing their way up this road and to the rear of the column's position. The command post was also placed here.

The second Lewis gun was placed at the point marked B, where it had a command of the road in front and to the east as far as the bend. Its fire to the west was somewhat restricted because of intervening rocks but it had an excellent command of the low

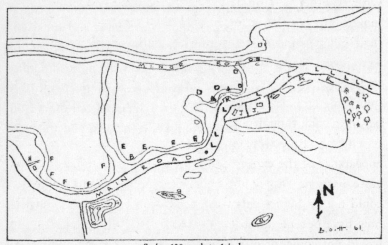

Scale—120 yards to 1 inch.

A: 1st Lewis Gun.   B: 2nd Lewis Gun.
C: Block on minor road controlled by fire from D.
D: No 1 Section   E: No 2 Section
F: No. 3 Section   G: No. 4 Section
H: Block of car to be placed when enemy approach was signalled. Controlled by fire.
J: Cottages.   K: Dead ground where enemy took cover.
L: Lorries.

ground to the south. No. 2 section were placed in position along here at either side of the gun.

No. 3 section were in position on the rocks immediately west and also acted as flankers at the western end. Here a temporary block ready to be pulled across the road on news of enemy approach was covered by this section.

No. 4 section were placed on the isolated rocks to the south and had a field of fire extending from the western cottage to the temporary block.

An observation post was placed on Rahoonagh Hill, an elevated position about one mile to the south having a view of the road four miles to the east and two miles to the west. Messages were to be flag-signalled to the position. The stage was now set.

Long Period of Waiting

On every other day from 18 February until 25 February the column moved into position at dawn, waited all day, and moved out to their billets some miles away when darkness fell. Instructions were issued to the men that on no account were they to show themselves to passing traffic, and after the first few hours spent in improving and camouflaging positions a long monotonous wait began in cold, though dry, wintry weather. This was not without its effect as time wore on and as day succeeded day with no appearance of the expected convoy, a feeling of disappointment arose, carrying with it the belief that as the column's activities could not be hidden from the countryside, the enemy must by now have become aware of its being in position and therefore would not come, or else would come in such force as to make the column's position dangerous. Among some this bred a certain carelessness and contempt which was to have a disastrous effect on the result of the fight.

Fighting Opens

As on previous days the column moved into position before dawn on 25 February, the signallers leaving for the observation post at the same time. Through a miscalculation these men did not reach the observation post until after the fighting had opened shortly after 8 a.m. and consequently the first intimation of enemy approach was received from the eastern flank when the first lorry passed the cross.

Every man was at once on the ready at his firing position. Everything was quiet. Each man waited for the signal to fire which was to come from the western end when the first lorry had reached this point thus enveloping within the position the entire convoy. There was one man, however, not at his post. This man had slipped unobserved across the road from his position to the western cottage a few minutes before the enemy were signalled, and now when he heard their approach unthinkingly rushed for his position. He was of course seen by the occupants of the leading lorry who opened fire on him as he was climbing to his post. The lorry pulled up, the firing bringing the others to a halt as well. The leading lorry's position was now at the bend below the western cottage and four more lorries were between this and the cross. The five remaining lorries were halted east of the cross and out of sight and one of these immediately turned and raced back to Macroom from whence an urgent message was wirelessed for reinforcements.

When the Auxiliaries opened fire at the man running from the cottage, fire was not immediately returned by the column as there persisted the faint hope that the lorries would proceed further into the position and so become more vulnerable but when the occupants began to dismount it was no longer withheld and some of the enemy began to drop while others raced for the cottages and the dead ground marked K. Three hostages who were in the lorries did likewise.

The forward Lewis gun at point marked A, with No. 1 section

at point marked D, together with about ten rifles of No. 4 section, were the only arms able to bear on the enemy at this juncture. The remaining Lewis gun with the arms of the other sections did not come into play until later as the road north and east from the bend below the cottage was hidden from their view. In all one Lewis gun, twenty-two Rifles and four shot-guns were in action at this vital stage and the presence of the hostages jumbled up with the Auxiliaries in the mad scramble for cover had a disturbing effect on the fire of the attackers. The Lewis gun too, which was of the small Aero type, jammed at a critical time and was out of action during the rest of the engagement.

The occupants of the lorries east of the cross deployed to positions along the fences of the road and a grove adjoining and remained mostly inactive during the ensuing struggle through they were able to prevent the encirclement of their positions.

Fire was now directed by No. 1 section against the front windows and door of the western cottage and also against the position held by the Auxiliaries in the dead ground along the fences, this being promptly returned. In the meantime Nos 2 and 3 sections were swung around across the minor road to a position on the hillside east of No. 1's position in an effort to encircle the entire enemy force. Owing to the nature of the ground which sloped gently towards the road, it was not found possible in view of enemy fire, to come closer than five hundred yards, and fire was opened at this range.

No. 4 section at the same time deployed to line the fence immediately south of the western cottage and fire was poured in through the rear window. It was found impossible to bring fire to bear on the windows and door of the other cottage owing to the fences commanding them being under enemy fire at both sides.

The main volume of the attacker's fire was therefore directed against the western cottage at very close range in an effort to wear down the resistance and capture it. This task fell to Nos 1 and 4 sections, the other sections from their more distant positions preventing the enemy to the east from coming to the occupants' aid. The Auxiliaries within however fought bravely back and it was only after a considerable time that their resistance weakened and finally seemed to cease entirely.

Reinforcements Arrive

At this critical juncture it was felt that the surrender of the cottage was at hand, this view being supported by the evidence of the hostages within who were afterwards questioned. Military reinforcements to the number of some hundreds now began to arrive and to deploy in an effort to envelop the entire position north of the road. This force, who came from Ballincollig, was afterwards joined by parties from Bandon and Killarney who endeavoured to link up from the south and west. Nothing remained but retreat.

Retreat

The order was given to Nos 1, 2 and 3 sections to fall back to the north-west and a message was sent to No. 4 section south of the road to retreat in the same direction. By a mischance, of which the day seemed to have had its share, it did not reach them for fully forty-five minutes later and this section continued to fight on unaware of the course events had now taken. After some time, becoming puzzled by the sound of firing from the north which appeared to be growing more distant while that from the cottage was again being renewed, a scout was sent northwards who returned with the messenger who had been detailed with the retreat instructions. This man not knowing their exact location was still looking for them. The section then fell back to the north-west coming under heavy enemy fire at several points and getting through the encircling movement in the nick of time. It was now after 12 noon, the fight having lasted approximately four hours.

They linked up with a portion of the column at Coomaguire, a glen about four miles to the north-west and the body then moved to Coomaclohy, about one mile farther on, to join the advance party which had reached there. On arriving they found a sharp engagement in progress between the advance party and the Killarney reinforcements who were trying to encircle them. On seeing the second body the enemy however, withdrew and the column then divided, one party moving to Coolea four miles to the south-west while the other tramped on twelve miles to the north-east to billet under the shadow of Mushera.

Result of Fight

While there were no casualties among the column the number of enemy dead has been put down at fourteen, including Lieutenant Sodie and the Auxiliary O/C – Major Grant. There were fourteen likewise wounded among the Auxiliaries and two among the military in the brush at Coomaclohy.

The loss in morale was even greater as British forces rarely ventured into this district again except in very large numbers, exceeding at times 2,000 men.

Lessons of Fight

There is a saying that it is easy to be wise after the event and this of course is true, but if we today are to derive any benefit from the lesson of this fight we must point out the reasons for its failure to achieve its full objective. They are as follows:

(a) Breakdown of observation post. This was a major calamity, as if it had functioned properly timely warning of enemy approach would have been given to the column, thus enabling a check to be made that all men were at their posts. The man in the cottage incident would never have happened and the advantage of surprise would have been held intact.

In extenuation of this lapse the Auxiliaries were never before known to leave Macroom so early, the usual time of departure of the convoys being 9 to 10 a.m. They were at the position shortly after 8 a.m. The signallers were at their post at about the same time but too late to be of use.

(b) Man away from this position. It would be unfair to apportion blame to anyone but to the man himself, firstly, for leaving his post, and, secondly, for running from the cottage with the certainty of enemy detection. No better way could be found to neutralise the element of surprise.

(c) Failure to arrange for temporary block, covered by fire, on road between ambush position and Macroom in order to prevent enemy reinforcements being summoned. Vital even if (a) and (b) did not occur. With large enemy convoys there is always the danger that the full number of lorries may not be enveloped within the position and any outside will most certainly fly for aid. There is also the possibility of an armoured car being with the convoy whose return may not be so easy to prevent by rifle fire alone. As (a) and (b) occurred the ambush could not have entirely succeeded but there is every reason to believe that had reinforcements not arrived, the occupants of the western cottage would have surrendered.

(d) The Auxiliary Force attacked were entirely on the defensive and fought as well as could be expected but the reinforcements when they arrived certainly erred in not pressing home at once the advantage which numbers and equipment gave them.

If they had done this, the section south of the road, isolated from the remainder of the column for forty-five minutes, during which time the military dominated the position, would never have got through them alive. God be praised that they did. And so ends the story of Ballyvourney.

Step Together

by M.J. Barry

Step together – boldly tread,
Firm each foot, erect each head,
Fixed in front be every glance –
Forward at the word 'advance' –
Serried files that foes may dread,
Like the deer on mountain heather,
Tread light,
Left right –
Steady, boys, and step together!

Step together – be each rank
Dressed in line, from flank to flank,
Marching so that you may halt
'Mid the onset's fierce assault,
Firm as is the rampart's bank
Raised the iron rain to weather –
Proud sight!
Left, right –
Steady, boys, and step together!

Step together – be your tramp
Quick and light – no plodding stamp;

Let its cadence, quick and clear,
Fall like music on the ear;
Noise befits not hall or camp –
Eagles soar on silent feather;
Tread light,
Left, right –
Steady, boys, and step together!

Step together – self-restrained,
Be your march of thought as trained,
Each man's single powers combined
Into one battalioned mind,
Moving on with step sustained;
Thus prepared, we reck not whether
Foes smite,
Left, right –
We can think and strike together.

RATHCOOLE AMBUSH

by Captain P. O'Brien, Infantry Corps

In the summer of 1921 I was operations' officer for the western area, Cork No. 2 Brigade, governing the first five battalions, and embracing Millstreet, Newmarket, Charleville, Kanturk, Mallow. Enemy military forces occupied Buttevant, Ballyvonare, Charleville, Mallow, Kanturk, Newmarket; and a strong force of Auxiliaries held Mount Leader, Millstreet.

At a Millstreet battalion council meeting in May it was decided to attack this Auxiliary force. Millstreet battalion headquarters at this time were in a well-concealed hut by the banks of the Blackwater at Drishane Beg, and from here all enemy movements could be really observed and recorded.

We ascertained that the Auxiliaries got their supplies at Banteer railway station, that they travelled to Banteer, via Rathcoole three days one week, two days the next; that they usually made the trip between 11 a.m. and 3 p.m.; that they made two trips on Tuesdays, between 9.30 and 11 a.m., and between 4.30 and 6.30 p.m. In twelve days' observation the only variation noticed was in the strength of parties travelling. The weakest convoy consisted of two armoured tenders, with ten men, a Lewis gun and grenades in each, and travelling about four hundred yards apart. The strongest had six tenders, similarly equipped, and covered about one and a quarter miles.

At this time a number of men from the local battalions had been trained in the construction and use of landmines. They were ordered to collect all explosive material in the area, and convert it into landmines, as we had decided that these would be the most effective means of disabling the enemy's armoured lorries. We then made a final check on the position of each lorry along the route when the lorry was at a given point.

We decided to strike on the evening of 16 June, because by our reckoning the enemy would make two trips that day, and the evening would give our men a better chance of scattering to their various retreats afterwards. About six hundred yards south of the ambush point there was a pine wood from which the men could quickly occupy action stations, and from which they could study, during the day, the enemy's travel formation and lie of the land.

On 14 June, despatches were sent to the 2nd, 3rd, 4th and 5th battalions, instructing the commanding officers to send all their riflemen on the night of 15 June. Despatches travelled by a cycle relay system, and on the night of 15 June the attacking party assembled.

Our total strength was one hundred and forty men, sixty-one riflemen, fifty shot-gun men; a Hotchkiss gun team of three; fourteen engineers armed with revolvers, and in charge of seven landmines which we had made. Four battalion staff officers, six signallers, and two first aid men completed the party.

The main attacking position was a point midway between Rathcoole and Cork Hill, the road here running between the Blackwater on the north side and the pine wood which was our base on the south. We organised the men in ten sections, eight of which were to be on the southern side of the road and two on the northern side. A section was to cover each mine position; six on the southern, and one, at Drishane Beg, on the northern side, with its eastern flank protected by five picked riflemen. One section was detailed to protect the east and west flanks of the main position. The local men, who knew the ground thoroughly, were distributed among the various sections.

At dawn on the 16 June we held a practice occupation of action stations; examined the lines of retreat from each position; and withdrew to the pine wood base. The engineers laid the landmines in their pre-arranged places. Dry weather, and the plentiful dust consequent, made it easy to camouflage the leads.

In the pine wood, the plan of attack was detailed to the section leaders as follows: mines to be numbered one to seven, from west to east. The enemy to be unmolested on the outward journey to Banteer. If this journey took place before 11 a.m. – it would indicate a repeat trip in the late afternoon, in which case the attack would be delayed till the homeward journey then. The rear lorry to be attacked first, the mines being so placed that there was little danger of the first lorry being clear of the mined zone by then. A close-up attack would not be practicable and it was explained that the possibility of capturing enemy equipment was slight, and that our main object was to inflict what casualties we could and get away under cover with the least possible loss. Attacking posts were at points varying from forty to one hundred and forty yards from the mines.

The men were now ordered to rest, while the local companies deployed as scouts all round us, with instructions to block all roads at the sound of the first explosion.

At 10.30 a.m. the enemy's approach was signalled from the west, and the convoy of three lorries passed towards Banteer, returning shortly afterwards. This gave such men as were awake a good chance to study the position of the lorries in relation to the mines and themselves. People from neighbouring houses provided food, in spite of the fact that they were well aware of our intentions, and the consequent danger to themselves and their homes.

About 4.30 p.m. the Auxiliaries again passed in from the west, this time in four lorries. The sections now moved quietly into position, and prepared for action on the return of the enemy. At 6 p.m. the lorries were sighted returning from the east, and while we kept under cover, they passed into their ambush position.

Number seven mine was exploded as fourth lorry reached it. The lorry stopped, disabled, and fire was opened immediately by the covering section. This section had the Hotchkiss gun with them, although frequent stoppages made it relatively useless, and finally it failed completely. Very little fire was returned from the lorry, and at least half its crew were incapacitated in the first minute of the engagement.

By now the first lorry had passed over number three mine, and, on the explosion of number seven had turned to come to the assistance of number four lorry. Number three mine was fired as the lorry re-crossed it and put it out of action. The majority of its crew were hit by the covering fire as they tried to leave, the remainder took cover under the damaged lorry and opened fire with rifles and Lewis gun against us.

The enemy's position now was that their number one and four lorries were out of action; number two and three were trapped between these and intermediate mines at the same time. They made no attempt, however, to move the undamaged lorries, but seemed content to cover the disabled cars from where they were. Our sections covering mines four, five and six engaged these lorries by rifle fire, and the enemy attempted a charge from the third lorry, combined with a flanking movement along the road from number two. This was effectively checked by shot-gun fire, and by exploding number five mine as the flanking party was passing over it.

All the enemy's Lewis guns were still in action; and our ammunition was running out. There seemed no possibility of capturing any material, so we signalled the retreat. Some confusion arose here, and the leaders had difficulty in keeping the men to the covered routes of retreat. However, the southern sections eventually assembled in the pine-wood without casualties and soon afterwards we were informed that the northern sections had withdrawn across the Blackwater with equal success.

All told, the fight lasted about fifty minutes, and, whilst no war material was captured at the time, we achieved our object in inflicting casualties upon the enemy, and in shaking his morale; while at the same time we strengthened the confidence of our own men, both in their own ability, and in the efficiency of the landmine, of which they had heard bad reports previously.

Ammunition was scarce in those days, as we were dependent for our supplies on captured enemy munitions. This engagement greatly depleted our stocks, we entered it with only forty rounds per rifle and two hundred and fifty for the Hotchkiss gun. Next day, a reconnaissance party from the column went back to scout the ambush post, and collected 1,350 rounds of .303 which the enemy had lost in evacuating his damaged lorries and casualties in the darkness of the previous night.

During this period it was not possible to keep large columns mobilised, therefore it was necessary to have well organised local units. This system enabled the columns to mobilise speedily, and at the same time function as a scouting network, with a constant eye on enemy movements.

Had it not been for these units, I have no hesitation in saying that the active service units could not have carried on. They established a tradition which the modern LDF might well follow, and which it will, I have no doubt, admirably maintain. It is in order to enable both branches of LDF to compare their position today with that of the IRA then that I have written this account of the ambush, and I suggest that it might be used as the basis of discussions, among groups, on the tactics employed, their strong and weak points, and how they would operate in modern conditions. If used in this way, the account of any engagement of the War of Independence can prove both interesting and instructive, especially if applied to the local terrain.

CAPTURED AT MIDLETON

by Commandant M. Kearney, Infantry Corps

A British Cycle Patrol was captured near Midleton, County Cork, on Saturday evening, 5 June 1920.

The patrol consisted of one RIC constable and twelve British soldiers including two Corporals. Their armament comprised one long Webley revolver and eighteen rounds of ammunition in possession of the Constable while each soldier carried a service rifle and fifty rounds. The capture was made about nine o'clock in the evening, one and a half miles west of Midleton, and on the main road to Cork.

Midleton is a town about midway between Cork city and Youghal, on the main road, roughly fifteen miles from the city. Prior to the Anglo-Irish War, Midleton was not a garrison town and the first occupation occurred about three weeks prior to this period when a detachment of the Essex Regiment arrived there and took up their quarters in an old disused factory which was situated in the northern end of the town, about one hundred and fifty yards from the RIC barracks. Its occupation by the military henceforth frustrated any attempt of the IRA to capture the RIC barracks.

While the Essex Regiment detachment were stationed in Midleton they went out frequently on patrol and always during the day. The eyes of the Volunteer officers followed such movements in every detail and as a result of the information gained this patrol was considered rather an easy prey and consequently a sharp lookout was kept for a suitable opportunity to attack the patrol. On 4 June, the Essex were relieved by a detachment of the Cameron Highlanders who, true to usage, carried on the same patrol system as followed by their predecessors.

On the evening of 5 June as Commandant Diarmuid Hurley, officer commanding 4th Battalion, 1st Cork Brigade, and another officer named Tadhg Manley were having a casual stroll, they were informed by two boy scouts who had been specially detailed to watch the movements of the enemy, that the patrol consisting of one RIC Constable and twelve soldiers, had gone out the Fermoy Road. This information was received at about 7.45 p.m. Fast thinking was necessary and Commandant Hurley immediately decided on a plan of action. He assumed that since the patrol went out by this road that they would return by the main road via Carrigtwohill.

He had a short consultation with Manley to whom he outlined his plan for the capture of the patrol on the return journey.

He sent one of the scouts to Carrigtwohill with instructions to watch the approach of the patrol to that town. When he saw it coming on to the main road and turning for Midleton he was to return immediately with that information to Ballyanan crossroads where Commandant Hurley would be.

He sent the second scout to mobilise every available Volunteer at Ballyanan crossroads with the instructions that any of them who could procure revolvers immediately were to do so. Otherwise they were to move out to the rendezvous with all possible speed and without arousing suspicion.

He had no time to get sufficient arms. So he had to depend solely on surprise effect for the successful carrying out of the job. He himself and Manley then went to the crossroads where in a short time they were joined by eight other Volunteers. Number two scout in the meantime directed any others he met to the mobilisation centre.

By this time, a sufficient number had arrived and Commandant Hurley told them of his intentions to capture the patrol and outlined his plan to them.

To deceive the enemy, they were to start playing a game of bowls, a Cork game in which pairs of competitors throw twenty-eight ounce iron balls along the roads. At important matches large numbers of spectators may be scattered over hundreds of yards of road. Commandant Hurley detailed the men to their various positions on the road, he and Manley taking up positions in the rear. He told them that a scout would arrive before the patrol to give warning of its approach. The patrol would be allowed to pass through until the head reached him and Manley who would then rapidly fire a few shots as a signal for each Volunteer to rush the nearest soldier to him, throw him off his bicycle and snatch his rifle.

In the summer evenings a game of bowls in progress is a very common sight at east Cork. So that on this particular evening a game of bowls did not appear unusual. The game had proceeded only a short distance when the scout arrived from Carrigtwohill with the information that the patrol was on its way back travelling slowly at the rate of six to eight miles per hour.

Commandant Hurley instructed the Volunteers to close up so that his party would cover about forty yards of the road. A few minutes later the patrol coming down an incline some distance away came into view of the leading Volunteers. Having thus a good view of the patrol, they were able to estimate roughly the space the patrol occupied on the road so that they were able to adjust their own distance to meet the situation. Coming to the bottom of the hill the patrol was lost to view for a while owing to shorter bend on the road, and on again coming into the straight they saw the Volunteers. Now the RIC man was at the head of the party and knowing the customs and pastimes of the area he immediately concluded that a harmless game of bowls was in progress.

When the patrol duly appeared, the Volunteers moved to the side of the road to allow them pass, as it were. They passed on until the RIC man reached Commandant Hurley and Manley when the latter two immediately fired a few rapid shots.

This was the signal for action and immediately the Volunteers rushed the patrol, now in a state of confusion as a result of the shots, hurled them off their bicycles and grabbed their rifles.

The surprise was complete, the soldiers made no resistance and the whole operation lasted only about a minute. The confusion among the patrol was increased owing to the fact that on coming down the hill the cyclists closed in on each other, so that when rushed on, they were practically all thrown off together and one or two who were not, threw aside their bicycles and put up their hands.

The job was over but danger still overhung this daring party of men. Being on the main road with military lorries likely to come along at any moment, no time could be lost in getting the valuable capture of rifles and ammunition away and accordingly a passing motor car was commandeered and the prize of the evening was conveyed to safety. The soldiers and RIC man with their bicycles were marched down a side road from where, after a short time, they were let go to make their way back to barracks bearing the news of their sad experience. The cycles were thrown inside the fence as it was considered too difficult to conceal them at the time owing to numerous raids in the area.

Immediately the patrol arrived in barracks two lorries filled with troops left for the scene of the hold-up, presumably to search for the ambushers who had by this time cleared away to safety. The military searched some houses in the vicinity, giving a rough time to any civilians whom they met. They returned to barracks about 11.30 p.m. only to retrace their steps on foot and in greater strength. When they failed to get any information as to the ambushers they started firing in all directions as was usually the case under such circumstances.

The RIC man on returning to barracks related his experience to his comrades, so that on hearing the firing and not knowing that the military were responsible for it, they came to the conclusion that an attack was being made on their own quarters. Consequently, they too, started firing and with the result that both parties kept up the firing for over a half an hour before either party realised that they had nothing to fear except from themselves.

Conclusion

There are a few very useful lessons to be learned from this very singular incident:

1. The first is the great importance of getting accurate information an getting it at the right time. If the information from the scout happened to be delayed for a further half an hour, then the capture of this patrol could not have taken place.

    The same applies to definite information received from the scout. Not alone did he know that the patrol went out but he knew the exact route taken by it, which enabled Commandant Hurley to exactly fix on a definite 'hold up' position and get his men there in time.

2. Quick Decision.

    Commandant Hurley had very little time in which to decide his plan of action. He was possessed of a very active brain and he visualised at once what was required to meet this situation, and when he made a decision there was no going back of it.

3. The originality of the plan adopted to carry out the job, which, as has been seen, proved very successful.

4. The Value of Surprise.

    In this case there was very little time available to collect sufficient arms, and Commandant Hurley in their absence had to depend entirely on the effect of surprise. Here again his judgement was correct.

FUN OF THE FAIR

by Commandant J. Barrett, Artillery Corps

In 1920 a company of British infantry was stationed in the old gaol, Ennis. In the butter market, about half a mile away, they had a transport park, over which a twenty-four hour guard, made up of one corporal and six men, was mounted. This guard was relieved between 5 and 6 p.m. daily, and the old guard marched back from the market to the gaol by an unvarying route.

Early in June the Volunteers decided to disarm one of these guard parties and capture its equipment. Men from the 1st, 2nd and 3rd Battalions of the Mid-Clare Brigade were selected and trained in the tactics to be followed. Nightly rehearsals were carried out in a wood near the town, when seven men, representing the military, marched over a route similar to that covered by the returning guard. The attacking party of twenty-one men was sub-divided into seven sections of three – one to each soldier. Number one of each section was to cover his soldier with a revolver, while number two secured the guard's rifle and number three silenced him by gentle throttling.

A week's rehearsal satisfied us that the men were confident and efficient and the only outstanding point was the choice of a date.

June 23rd was finally picked. It was the day of Spancelhill horse-fair, and the streets in the evening would be crowded with dealers and horses. Seven Volunteers were instructed to take their horses

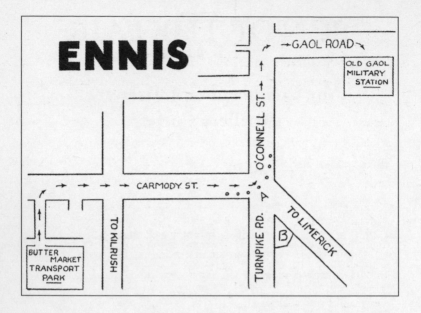

to the junction of O'Connell Street, Limerick Road and Carmody Street, and to hold them there at intervals of twenty-two yards, in the positions marked on the map. The attacking party would pretend to be buying these horses, thus at once avoiding police attention and occupying the best striking position.

The 'horse-dealers' commenced buying negotiation at 5.30 p.m. on 23 June, while their commanding officer stood in the middle of the crossroads in the role of interested spectator (A on map). From this spot he could see the approaching guard two hundred yards away.

About 5.55 p.m. they were sighted, and the horse dealing came to a crescendo. As they came abreast of the 'dealers', the commanding officer signalled the attack by a long blast on a whistle. The British corporal offered some resistance, and had to be quieted by a punch. The remainder were completely overwhelmed by the swiftness and spontaneity of the attack, and gave no trouble.

This really active part of the operation lasted rather less than two minutes, during, which time seven men, armed with rifles and fixed bayonets were disarmed, and horse dealing concluded for the day. Having disarmed the soldiers, the Volunteers marched them into D'Arcy's yard (B on map), where their web equipment, steel helmets and three hundred and fifty rounds of ammunition were taken. Three waiting cars took the captured material to Kilmorane, two miles outside Ennis, and the attack party dispersed in ones and twos.

Many of the townspeople witnessed the ambush and knew the men engaged in it; and to their credit be it said that although most of them disagreed with the Volunteers' policy, no information was given to the British authorities. Raids began immediately, but met with no success.

Around this period, much British propaganda was in circulation to the effect that the Volunteers had not the courage to attack in the open.

The moral affect of this ambush, staged in the middle of a country town on a fair day, was therefore at least as great as its military effect.

The captured rifles were subsequently used with much success, notable in the capture of Ruan barracks, in October 1920.

THE MALLOW RAID

by B.O.J.

Attack and capture of Mallow Military Barracks

On the night of 27 September 1920, the 4th Cork Brigade column, under the leadership of Liam Lynch and Ernie O'Malley, had to be scouted into the Mallow town hall. This operation continued until the early hours of the morning of 28 September, and was entrusted to the members of the Mallow company who were conversant with the less noticeable approaches. There were military as well as Tan barracks in the Town. Patrols from both were constantly patrolling the town and district. It was therefore imperative that strong scouting parties should keep both under observation and also the private houses of the RIC. The slightest hitch would have spoiled the whole operation.

The hall was situated in the centre of the town, having the Tan barracks fully covering its front fifty yards to the north, and the objective Military Barracks, two hundred yards to the rear south-west, with retreat to the east and west cut off with houses intervening. Therefore it can be gathered that careful and proper scouting was essential. The whole attacking party having arrived at the hall, their temporary headquarters, outposts were placed in positions. The outside appearance of the hall gave no indication of what was housed within its walls.

The remainder of the company required was now mobilised, and allotted to their various, posts. Mallow was an important centre in North Cork, within easy reach of the big military barracks at Buttevant, Ballyvonare and Fermoy. Also being the railway junction for the south it was fed by lines from Kerry, Waterford, and Cork for Dublin. As it had one of the most important post offices between Cork and Dublin, thousands of telegraph and telephone wires had to be cut at the given time. This required a big number of men. Then provision had to be made for the conveyance of the material if successful in the capture of the barrack. Should the plans fail a hasty retreat would be necessary. Petrol could not be openly purchased without arousing some suspicion, and had to be got from the dump which was situated only two hundred yards from the military barracks. That in itself had to be done very carefully.

Motor cars were then commandeered and armed guards placed over the owners, their families and servants until the 'All Clear' was given. All roads leading to the town were carefully scouted.

Men had to be in their position before the inhabitants were astir. The military who left the barracks for exercise had to be kept under observation, because if they made an unexpected return, they would cut off the attacking party.

The main retreat led through the Mallow town park to the Blackwater Bridge main road. This bridge, the exercising party had also to return by. It was the only bridge to the town from the south. The military at that particular period were patrolling the country by motor-lorry, so that at any moment they could be expected. Therefore the bridge was heavily guarded, and the scouts watching the exercising field had to keep in touch with the storming-party and bridge out-post, as the field was within gunshot of the barracks.

The military who left for the purpose of exercising were mounted, being the 17th Lancers. It is therefore evident that the slightest hitch would have meant disaster to the attacking party. Men were also placed at advantage points to count the military that left in order that the exact strength of the defenders were known to the storming party. The day was yet young, dawn having but broken.

Success or failure depended on two men who were working in the barracks. It was entirely on their information that the bridge column, outposts, etc. now found themselves ready to strike.

These two men take with them this morning the brigade quartermaster. He is supposed to be the clerk of works, to look over the work they had been engaged in for some time previously as painter and carpenter, but this morning in place of the rule, saw, paint brush and blueprint, their pockets hold a pair of revolvers each. They enter the barracks.

The exercising party prepare and leave for their usual training field, passing by the town hall under the muzzles of the rifles which are trained on the Tan barracks. They are carefully counted as they pass. Business has assumed its usual routine in the town, no armed men to be seen anywhere. The motor cars now move into waiting position, and military are now nearing the exercise field. The watchful scout is now signalling. They have arrived. The storming party led by scouts leave their temporary headquarters through the rear entrance and windows and advance at the double for the barracks.

Having arrived unnoticed they keep under cover. Ernie O'Malley knocks at the small gate, the unsuspecting sentry opens it. Before he has time to think, the rifle is snatched from his grasp.

The men already inside rushed and held up the guardroom. The sergeant in charge was about to train the machine gun on the main gate which was by now open. He failed to surrender when called upon and had to be shot. He would have annihilated the whole party as they were advancing through the open gateway only for the shot finding its mark so quickly.

The moment the gates were open, all communications were cut, and Mallow was isolated. The motor cars pulled into the barracks, all the military having been disarmed in the meantime, and locked in one large room. Willing hands quickly filled the cars with machine guns, rifles, revolvers and equipment of all kinds. The sergeant was temporarily bandaged and all that was possible was done for him. The retreat whistle was then sounded. The cars went on their way and the main body crossed the bridge safely. Trees were felled on all roads immediately hampering reinforcements, all outposts and the column safely retreated. So ended one of the greatest and one of the most successful raids during the whole campaign.

What are the lessons to be learned from this successful operations? Again as exemplified in previous articles in *An Cosantóir,* the element of surprise was of supreme importance. The sergeant with the machine gun might easily have wiped out the party if he had got a slight opportunity.

On what in turn did the achievement of surprise depend? It depended on information that was complete and up-to-date, on a thoroughness of preparation which took safeguards against all contingencies, on thorough scouting and observation up to the end and on a calm, businesslike determination in the actual carrying out of the operation.

1916 – DEFENCE OF MOUNT ST BRIDGE:
A CLASSIC OF STREET FIGHTING

by Commandant A. Thompson, GHQ

The defence of Mount Street Bridge was an outpost engagement during Easter Week 1916, carried out by Volunteers of the 3rd Battalion, Dublin Brigade. The battalion area was bounded on the north by the Liffey; on the west by O'Connell Street, Trinity College and Stephen's Green; and on the south by Leeson Street. Paralleled by Pearse Street (then Brunswick Street), Grand Canal Street and Lower Mount Street. Hence it will be seen that the main and most likely route of approach to be used by enemy reinforcements from Dún Laoghaire ran through the area and defences were planned accordingly.

Opening Operation

Offensive operations were begun at 12.30 on Easter Monday, 24 April, by the capture of the DSE railway, running east to Wicklow, precluding its use by the enemy. Battalion headquarters were established in Boland's Mill, main positions were taken up and outposts occupied, including Clanwilliam House, the School, 25

Northumberland Road, and Carisbrooke House. The fields of fire from these outposts covered two hundred, two hundred and fifty, and four hundred and fifty yards respectively. As well as covering reinforcements from Dún Laoghaire, these posts were relied on to hold the Beggar's Bush garrison to its barracks.

Strength of Outposts

On Wednesday 26 April, the strength and armaments of the outposts' forces was:

- Carisbrooke House: three Volunteers, two rifles, one revolver.
- 25 Northumberland Road: two Volunteers with two rifles.
- The School: three Volunteers, three rifles.
- Clanwilliam House: one section commander and six men, with a Lee Enfield, six Mausers and seven revolvers.
- Clanwilliam House had been fortified as far as possible by barricading all likely entrances with the furniture, strengthened by clay from the garden.

The Enemy Arrives

On the evening of 25 April, British transports disembarked the 178th and 176th Infantry Brigades at Dún Laoghaire. The following morning the 178th Brigade was formed into columns for the advance into the city. The 5th and 6th battalions, Sherwood Foresters, composed the left column, and, marching by Blackrock, Stillorgan, Donnybrook, arrived in Dublin unchallenged and in time to take part in the bitter fighting for the South Dublin Union. The right column, with the 7th and 8th Sherwood Foresters, followed the main road through Blackrock and Ballsbridge, and at about 12.30 their Advance Guard came along Northumberland Road.

Advance Guard Engaged

When they came abreast of Carisbrooke House the advance guard was fired on, and after replying to the fire, continued up Northumberland Road. Either the advance guard had prior information of the occupation of No. 25 or were becoming more cautious, for on reaching No. 25 they opened fire on the house. The defenders did not reply immediately, but held fire until the advance guard was directly opposite the school and almost at Mount St Bridge, with the head of the 7th battalion close on their tail.

The Fight

From Clanwilliam House and the school a well-directed and deadly fire was now poured into them taking them completely by surprise. No. 25's garrison simultaneously engaged the centre of the column. The enemy sought cover and replied with heavy fire on the occupied posts.

The fight now settled down to a pitched battle. Covering machine-gun fire was turned on Clanwilliam House while a bombing-party stormed No. 25. Lieutenant Malone and Seamus Grace, the two Volunteers in No. 25, fired as fast as they could load while the house shuddered with explosions as the grenades found their mark. Then a bomb got Lieutenant Malone, and Seamus Grace was left to fight alone over his comrade's body. Finally he could maintain his position no longer, and he escaped through the smoke. When the Foresters finally took the house they found one dead man in what was later described in despatches as 'a strongly held post'.

But Clanwilliam House remained and the fight from there was only beginning. After three hours fighting its defenders sustained

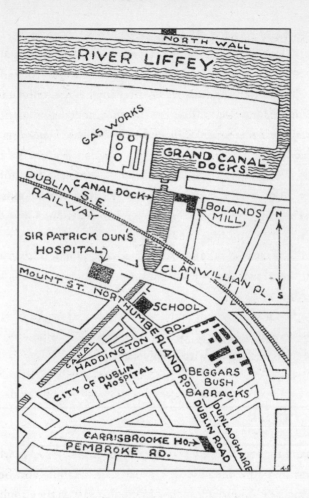

their first casualties, two Volunteers, one of them the section commander, being killed. The other posts having been now over-run, the concentrated fire of the enemy was brought to bear on the one remaining defensive position; this fire had cut the water piping and had carried away the stairs in rear of one of the windows.

Capture of the house was attempted by massed assaults under covering fire from rifles and grenades. The assaulting parties were repulsed, and repeated attacks only added to their already heavy losses. After a time attempts to storm the house were discontinued.

Only five men were left as the successive waves of attackers broke against Clanwilliam House. At about 5 p.m. they were reduced to four when Volunteer Murphy was killed.

Each window was now used alternately and a tailor's dummy found in the house was utilised at the undefended windows to draw fire away from the others. It lasted only a short time, but served its purpose.

The enemy also tried to advance by crawling along the street channel. The first man who showed himself was shot, and the others, by gathering round him, exposed themselves and became casualties. The Volunteers' enfilade fire, along the channel's well-defined line, ensured that if the first advancing enemy was not hit, one further down the line was, and this method of attack was also given up.

As the fight grew more intense, the defenders' rifles became red hot on several occasions. While they were laid aside to cool, the defence was carried on with revolvers.

The Finish

At 8 p.m. the four defenders were still successfully withholding the two enemy battalions, but now a party of a Royal Naval Reserve brought a one-pounder gun, mounted on a lorry, into action.

Incendiary shells from this gun and grenades started fires, which could not be controlled, in various parts of the house. Suffocating smoke swirled round the defenders, and it became obvious that the post was no longer tenable. They retired at 9 p.m. after nine hours continuous fighting.

Sir John Maxwell subsequently reported: 'In view of the opposition met with, it was not considered advisable to push on … that night, so at 11 p.m. the 5th South Staffordshire Regiment from the 176th Infantry Brigade, reinforced this column, and by occupying the positions gained, allowed the two battalions Sherwood Foresters to be concentrated on Ballsbridge.'

Compassionate Truces

The enemy casualties were such that fire ceased on both sides on two or three occasions to enable the medical service to carry away the dead and wounded. Such truces were honourably observed, the fight afterwards being resumed. The British War Office admitted two hundred and thirty-five killed and wounded, including twenty officers.

Analysis of the Engagement

The Volunteers' success was largely due to:

(1) Well-laid plans
(2) The choice of commanding positions disposed at the proper places.
(3) The proper fortification of positions.
(4) The withholding of fire until the last moment in order to effect surprise and demoralisation.
(5) Mutual confidence. This section had faith in their leader, in themselves, and in their cause. They succeeded in withstanding forces outnumbering them by over a hundred to one.
(6) The most profitable exploitation of firepower possible.
(7) Ingenuity, determination and foresight, as exemplified by the use of the tailor's model, the length the post was held, and the intelligent barricading of the post beforehand.

Contributory causes of the enemy's failure were:

(1) The advance guard did not carry out its duties thoroughly – when no fire was returned from No. 25 they neglected to search the house.

(2) When the main body closed in on top of the Advance Guard, they negatived [*sic*] its function – it ceased to be an advance guard, and became simply the head of a closely packed column.

Irish Times casualty list: One hundred and forty-two – seventy-three military and sixty-nine civilians, dealt with in Sir Patrick Dunn's hospital.

Brian O'Neill – quoting General Maxwell – 'Four officers were killed, fourteen wounded; other ranks two hundred and sixteen killed and wounded.'

O'Neill: 'One battalion detoured into Percy Place, which runs parallel with the canal on the south side and, sheltering behind the low canal wall, crept towards the bridge … The Volunteers could not stop the advance as long as the enemy lay behind the wall, but a steady fire was enough to render the attack impotent, for the attackers had to expose themselves when firing. The soldiers crept along Northumberland Road, crouching behind the stone steps of the houses as they fired. Then the officers would order a rush, and the nearer the rush approached Clanwilliam House, the greater were the casualties. After an hour of this sort of fighting the British contented themselves with long-range fire …'

> *In this supreme hour the Irish nation must by its valour and discipline and by the readiness of its children to sacrifice themselves for the common good, prove itself worthy of the august destiny to which it is call.*
> Proclamation of the Republic, 1916

THE MODREENY AMBUSH

by District Leader Seán Gaynor

At 4 a.m. one morning in May 1921, the active service unit of Tipperary No. 1 Brigade was roused from billets and, after a hurried breakfast, ordered to fall in.

The normal strength of the column, due to lack of rifles, was twenty men, armed with nineteen rifles, six revolvers and one automatic shot-gun; but on this morning the ranks were depleted by the absence of five men on sick leave, who had taken their rifles with them.

The total strength of the column on the morning in question, therefore, was fifteen men of all ranks and their armament consisted of fourteen rifles with fifty rounds for each, six revolvers with ten rounds for each and one automatic shot-gun with thirty cartridges. A further eight men from Cloughjordan company, armed with shot-guns, had been mobilised on the previous night, and fell in with the column.

As the officer commanding the column marshalled his twenty-two men, there was a look of expectancy on every face. The brigade O/C had arrived a few days previously and had had several consultations with the column commander – obviously there was something in the wind.

Judging by the strength of the column as it is marched away from billets no very big operation was contemplated, but it had become so difficult of late to lure the enemy from his strongly fortified positions that any kind of an engagement would be a relief. For months past the column had prepared ambushes for the enemy, but always he had failed to appear. Would there be better luck this time?

Marching at the head of the column, the brigade and column commanders discussed the forthcoming action. It appeared that some days previously the brigade staff had discovered that an enemy court was to be held in Cloughjordan on the following Friday. This is in itself was unusual and offered such possibilities that the brigade O/C had at once set out for the column. Arriving there he had the report confirmed by the Borrisokane company intelligence officer, who sent word that a cycle column of thirteen RIC men were going from Borrisokane to Cloughjordan on Friday morning to attend a court.

The handling of this enemy column looked like a job that the fifteen men in the active service unit could easily manage, but in order to provide scouts and runners eight men were picked from the local company. In the level country between Borrisokane and Cloughjordan there is no really good position for an ambush, but in view of the enemy strength an ideal position was not considered necessary. At Modreeny, midway between the two towns, a fairly good position for a quick stand-up fight was selected.

At the points selected there was cover from view afforded by whitethorn hedges, and a good field of fire to cover the road. Rising ground to the north afforded a view to Borrisokane for about half a mile outside the ambush position, and here two semaphore signallers were placed.

The sketch gives an indication of the appearance of the road and the positions occupied the IRA. The main position was at 'A' where there was an old shed and a rick of straw. A gateway and low wall faced the road to 'J' which was straight for three hundred yards. The second important position was at 'B' where again a gateway and low

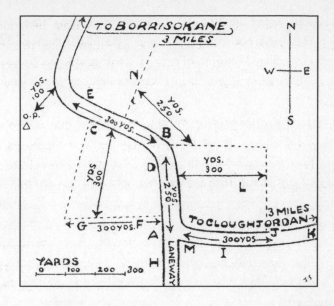

wall faced the road from 'B' to 'A'. The plan of attack was to let the cycle column through until the last man passed through the corner at 'B'. Then on the sound of the whistle, fire would be opened from 'A' to 'J' and from 'B' to 'A'.

Arriving at the position at 5.30 a.m. the following dispositions were made: five men armed with rifles under an NCO were instructed to open fire on the road from 'B' to 'A' on the sound of the whistle.

The NCO was informed of the plan of operations and was told to use his own discretion in any situation that might arise after the fight had started.

There were low whitethorn hedges on both side of the road from 'B' to 'A' and a rifleman posted behind the low hedge at 'L' and another at 'F' were instructed to prevent the enemy from leaving the road. Four men with rifles and two with shot-guns were posted from 'A' to 'B'. The riflemen were instructed to deal with those at close range in either direction. The remaining men with shot-guns were placed inside the fence at 'I' to deal with any of the enemy getting over the fence and to cover the flank of the main position. Two riflemen were kept in reserve at 'A'. Two signallers were sent to OP to signal enemy approach and strength to column commander at 'A'.

Everything was now ready and the only setback to be anticipated was the possibility of the enemy cyclists failing to turn up.

The time seemed long from 5.30 to 10 o'clock and still there was no sign of the enemy. The next half hour passed without result, and suddenly two cyclists were signalled as approaching, and then two more, and after a slight interval, two more cyclists. The enemy was coming. The next messages from the signaller read: one car, then another car, then four cyclists and, finally, after a pause, one lorry. This was disquieting. A quick calculation, allowing four to each car and twelve to the lorry, gave a minimum enemy strength of forty to the column's twenty-two. The men were poorly armed for a job of this magnitude and in the position occupied they had to win in order to get away without heavy loss. They could, however, lie low and let the enemy pass as the cover was good. The brigade and column commanders looked at one another and the same question was in both their eyes – will we attack? A nod from both settled the matter – they would attack.

Two reserve riflemen – the column commander was one – moved to 'C' to protect flank and rear. The six enemy cyclists passed the bend at 'A' and were allowed to continue on their way – the original plan of attack being adhered to with slight variations. The whistle however would not go until the first car at 'A'. There was no time to give any fresh order to the men of 'B'. So the column continued waiting for the first car. It seemed a long time coming – the six cyclists would be soon out of view. Then the whistle went and simultaneously the sound of rifle fire. The riflemen carried out their orders and four of the six cyclists were put out of action. The shot-guns riddled the first car killing three of the occupants. The other cars pulled up and the occupants and the remainder of the cyclists took cover under the hedges at both sides of the road. Here they were subjected to heavy fire from the position at 'B', while the men at 'F' and 'L' prevented them from getting over the hedge. All the enemy forces with the exception of those in the lorry were inside the ambush position. The lorry containing military was outside the trap and now constituted the chief danger. The soldiers dismounted and the lorry was sent back for reinforcements. The fence on the road from 'C' to 'D' was a low stone wall and it was now manned by military threatening the rear of the column. They had a plentiful supply of rifle grenades which they used freely though fortunately without effect. They made several attempts to get over the wall to rush the rear of the position at 'A' but the two men at 'G' as well as the man at 'F' kept up such an accurate fire that all these attempts failed.

In the meantime furious fighting continued at 'A'. The enemy between 'B' and 'A' made attempts to rush the position and suffered heavily each time. It soon became obvious that something had gone wrong with the section at 'B'. Had they been still holding their position nothing could have lived on the stretch of road from 'B' to 'A' but there was no sound from them and after half an hour's fighting a position of stalemate had been reached. The men with shot-guns at 'I' were moved into the corner at 'M' but the range was too long to force a decision.

It was now discovered that the military had taken up a position behind the fence at 'N', thus making the position of the section at 'B' untenable. This section had to withdraw and take up a defensive position to prevent the main position from being out-flanked.

The column had cut it pretty fine with regard to time as there were strong forces of 'Tans in barracks, four miles on either side. The military garrison at Nenagh was only eight miles to the south and the military garrison at Birr, fourteen miles to the north-east. The lorry had been gone half an hour for reinforcements. Repeated demands to the enemy to surrender had met with no response and there was no alternative but to withdraw. Having collected all the arms and ammunition on the road from 'A' to 'J' the retreat was ordered. This was carried out in a southerly direction for a short distance and then, swinging sharply to the north-east, the road was crossed beyond 'K', and the column marched in the general direction of Birr.

The results of the engagement were as follows:

Enemy killed, 4; enemy wounded 14. IRA casualties, nil. Rifles captured by IRA, 4. Ammunition captured by IRA, 200 rounds.

THE MOLOTOV 'COCKTAIL'

Only the most stout-hearted men should be chosen for the use of this weapon. They must be highly trained in the use of ground and in stalking. Most tanks have some blind spot from which they find it difficult or impossible to produce fire. There also seem to be some possibilities in the use of the smoke grenade thrown by infantry to allow the 'cocktail' throwers to get close to their objective.

The position chosen for the use of 'cocktails' should have the following points:

(a) Be in advance of a roadblock or trench at a point where the tank would most likely stop on locating the obstacle.

(b) Have cover from the direction of enemy advance so that a tank in rear may not be able to attack the 'cocktail' throwers.

(c) Afford cover to the 'cocktail' throwers.

(d) If possible, be on a higher level than the road.

(e) When the position is chosen, sufficient 'cocktail' material should be supplied to the throwers.

(f) A pit should be dug to afford protection for the 'cocktails' from dampness.

(g) Sharpshooters should be posted to deal with reconnaissance parties, motorcyclists.

The procedure would be as follows: the tanks, proceeded by two or three motor-cyclists, approach the road-blocks. The sharpshooters shoot the motor-cyclists, but take care not to expose themselves to the tanks. Without the motor-cyclists, the tanks are to some extent blinded and when the attempt is made to advance they come up against the road-block and are forced to halt. Fire is then opened by a concealed light automatic or concealed riflemen to force the tanks to close down all portholes. The fire is then stopped by signal and the 'cocktail' throwers go into action. Once the tank has been set on fire, further fuel in the shape of more 'cocktails' is rapidly added. Should the tanks remain stationary after the motor-cyclists have been dealt with, the 'cocktail' throwers will go forward and attack them. If any artillery pieces are near, they will rush forward to a direct fire position and engage the tanks.

'Cocktail' throwing demands cool courage – a hot-headed man will expose himself prematurely and either lose his life or give away the position. In Spain this work was done by chosen volunteers.

RAID ON KILMALLOCK RIC BARRACKS

by Lieutenant M. Guirke, Cavalry Corps (reprinted from *An t-Óglach*)

By the spring of 1920, the campaign against RIC barracks was well under way and was successfully fulfilling its two-fold purpose of loosening enemy's hold on the country and augmenting the arms of the Volunteers.

It was decided to attack and capture Kilmallock RIC barracks. It was discovered that the normal strength of the barracks consisted of two sergeants and eighteen men. The building was a very substantial one; and all the windows were steel shuttered and slotted to enable rifle to be fired through them. In addition to a plentiful supply of ammunition, the garrison was well provided with rifle, grenades and Mills bombs. In short, the police were in the position of an exceptionally strong military force with every prospect of holding out for days against even overwhelming numbers.

The barrack, however, had one drawback, of which great advantage could be taken by daring attackers. Situated in the main street of the village, it was a rather low, squat structure strongly built, but overlooked by higher buildings adjacent to it. This gave the attackers, provided they could occupy these buildings successfully, a dominant position over those in the barracks.

With regard to the movements of the garrison, it was learned that whilst normally the strength was two sergeants and eighteen constables, this number varied almost nightly. Individual RIC men came and departed by train on special plain clothes duty. Occasionally they came by Crossley tender. So that it was never possible to say accurately what was the strength of the garrison on a particular night. On the night of the attack the garrison consisted of twenty-eight men.

In our area service rifles were few; and for the attack on this stronghold the greatest difficulty was experienced in getting even thirty rifles. Our leader, Séan Forde, decided that the night of the attack was to be 27 May 1920. The rifles, some ammunition and all available shot-guns were dumped on the western side of Kilmallock, and the greater portion of ammunition, bombs and explosives was dumped on the eastern side.

It was too much to hope that so strong a barrack could be carried by a short, sharp attack. It would obviously have to be besieged. This constituted the greatest part of our task, because a protracted fight would certainly lead to the possibility of reinforcements coming to the relief of the garrison. Our force was too small for the risk to be lightly regarded.

All available help in the entire district was accordingly mobilised at 9 o'clock on the night of the attack, and all main roads, by-roads, and railway tracks for a radius of about fifteen miles around Kilmallock were rendered impassable for any form of traffic. A prodigious amount of labour went into this work, but it was cheerfully and effectively done, and it was well indeed that it was so, for the barrack proved a far tougher proposition than we had counted upon.

All preliminaries having been completed, the mobilisation of the attackers began. At 8 o'clock eighteen men from my battalion concentrated at Garryspillane crossroads, all in possession of bicycles, and proceeded to Kilmallock direct, to join forces with other detachments from West Limerick and East Clare.

Owing to the thoroughness of the obstructions over the roads our progress towards Kilmallock was very slow. The detachment I was with arrived in the town about 10.30 p.m., and linked up with the main body to the west of Kilmallock, under the command of Seán Forde.

About thirty men, each of whom was recommended by his local commander, were now specially selected, armed with the best of the rifles, given a plentiful supply of ammunition, and detailed for the direct attack on the barracks. The remaining men, to the number of about forty, armed with shot-guns and all sorts of miniature weapons, were detailed to guard minor entrances and exits.

Our detachment, that is to say, those detailed for the direct attack, was next divided into five sections, each choosing its own leader.

Each section received detailed instructions concerning the various buildings surrounding the barrack, which they were to occupy and fortify – Clery's Hotel fell to our lot.

This extensive building stood directly in front of the barrack and afforded an excellent commanding position, being about twice the height of the barrack. Our intelligence had reported the previous day that Clery's could not be entered either by front or rear so late at night, and in order to make sure of admission the following plan was adopted.

One of the IRA was detailed to proceed to Kilmallock by evening train in the guise of a commercial traveller, and book a bed for the night in Clery's. This would ensure having a man of our own inside to let us in; and it also meant that he would get a pretty good knowledge of the occupants and the interior arrangements.

This simple plan worked splendidly. The instant our section leader tapped gently at the door our comrade inside laid down the book he was reading and opened wide the door, thus enabling us to enter quietly and take possession.

Houses all round the barrack were by now occupied, and the work of fortifying them began. Each man barricaded the window allotted to him with whatever material was available. Needless to say, the material available was not ideal for the purpose, and but a sorry substitute for the steel shuttered windows opposite. But a high spirit of confidence animated us; and by 11.30 p.m. we were all at our posts, with loaded rifles at the ready, waiting with what patience we could for the signal to begin the attack.

About six paces from the gable-end of the barracks, facing south-west, another building towered above it. From the roof of the building our leader was to give three flashes of a lamp, which was the signal to begin the attack.

All eyes were now straining towards this point. There was no sign of life or activity from the barrack; and we seemed to have made our occupation of the surrounding houses without arousing any suspicions.

Suddenly from the roof top three flashes of light winked out into the night; and were instantly answered by the roar of thirty rifles. At the same moment our leader cast a fifty-six pound weight crashing through the slates of the barrack roof. Two other fifty-six pound weights followed in quick succession, their crashing noise passing almost unnoticed in the din of rifles and bursting bombs.

This unique method of breaking a fort was very effective, causing a large gaping hole in the roof. Into this opening our leader, from the roof, hurled bottle after bottle of petrol.

The bottles broke and saturated the roof with petrol. Then our leader hurled bombs into the breach. Each bomb burst with terrific force causing considerable damage but completely failing to set the roof on fire.

Meanwhile the fight was raging fiercely all round the barrack. The large garrison had manned every loop-hole and were returning a hot fire to our attack. It looked as if we would not succeed in forcing them either to surrender or evacuate. The bombing of the petrol-soaked roof, upon which great hopes had been set, did not appear to be working out, and unless some other means of reducing the structure of the building was brought into play it was evident that bomb and rifle fire would be unavailing.

It was under those conditions that the real genius of our leader rose to the occasion. He detailed a small party of those guarding the exits to proceed to a yard in the town where there was an American paraffin oil car. It was the tank-shaped type so commonly used in distributing supplies to country traders, and contained a huge quantity of paraffin oil. This car was now brought up the street, and with considerable difficulty and danger placed close to the barracks. By means of a hose the paraffin was now poured into the breach in the roof, for the best part of an hour. Then another Mills bomb hurled into the breach had the desired effect, and the roof burst into a blaze. Even after the roof had taken fire, the stream of paraffin was kept playing on the roof, with the result that in a few minutes it became a roaring furnace.

The battle for possession of the barracks raged without intermission from midnight to 2 a.m. At that hour our leader flashed out the 'cease fire' signal from his perch on the house-top. It was almost instantly obeyed by the attackers and the only sound was from the intermittent fire of the defenders.

It was a weird night, and one which the participants are never likely to forget – the smoke of burst bombs and the burning roof billowing around the building, the sudden comparative quiet after the fierce noise of the conflict, the red, hungry flame shooting skyward out of the doomed building.

The garrison was called on to surrender; but the reply was, 'No surrender', followed by a volley of rifle and grenade fire.

Instantly the three flashes of light for the 'open fire' winked out from the house-top and the battle was again in full swing. For upwards of three more hours the building – the fire of which was increasing every moment – was subjected to a continuous attack.

During all this time the defenders, who showed remarkable courage and pertinacity, directed their main efforts against Clery's Hotel. They endeavoured to make this position untenable by a continuous attack with rifle grenades. In this they were considerably handicapped by our elevated position and the fact that the street space between the two buildings was filled with dense smoke. Owing largely to these facts, I believe, they failed to get a singe one of their grenades in through any of the windows occupied by us. None the less our position was rather precarious. Grenade after grenade hit the front wall, dropped to the ground and burst with terrific force. These repeated concussions were causing considering damage to the lower position of the front of the hotel.

The fight had been waged for over five hours and the entire barrack was little better than a roaring furnace. The position of the defenders was hopeless, as it was quite impossible to remain any longer in the building.

Once more the 'cease fire' signal flashed out. Silence again took the place of conflict. The garrison, for the last time, were called upon to 'surrender'. Their answer was 'never', followed by a few shots.

The fight then recommenced and was continued up to about a quarter to six. About that hour the entire roof fell in, amidst frantic cheering from the attackers. Flames, sparks and clouds of smoke now shot skyward, giving a weird red tinge to the whole scene. The defenders had by this time made a dash to a small building in the yard of the barrack. This building, like the barracks, was fortified. In their fight they abandoned most of their bombs and ammunition, and the bursting of these within the burning building added to the din and clamour of the fight.

From this small building they put up a stubborn resistance. They fought the fight of heroes; and although we were engaged in a life and death struggle with them, we readily acknowledged the magnificent stand they made in face of an utterly hopeless situation.

Their retreat led to a change of our position also. We evacuated our former posts, and got into new ones at the rear without suffering any casualties, although it had now become fairly light.

The fact that the RIC had abandoned most of their reserve of ammunition in their flight from the barracks conferred no great advantage on us. We had begun our attack with a pitifully small supply of ammunition and bombs, and, after more than six hours' continuous fighting, our supplies were well nigh exhausted. Thus it was that, about 7 a.m., with daylight full across the country, our supplies of ammunition exhausted, and the danger of being trapped by heavy reinforcements, our leader was forced to sound the 'Retire'. We fired a parting volley and began our retirement.

We retired in good order across the country, leaving the barracks a smouldering ruin. Had the attack started half an hour earlier, or had we had another half-dozen bombs in our possession, we could have reduced the out-building and compelled the RIC to surrender, or die fighting in the open. However, we could, without exaggeration, claim that we had accomplished what we set out to do, namely, to reduce to ruins the enemy stronghold in the town of Kilmallock.

NATIONAL FREEDOM

'Like a divine religion, national freedom bears the marks of unity, of sanctity, of Catholicity, of apostolic succession. Of unity, for it contemplates the nation as one; of sanctity, for it is holy in itself and in those who serve it; of Catholicity, for it embraces all the men and women of the nation; of apostolic succession, for it, or the aspiration after it, passes down from generation to generation from the nation's fathers. A nation's fundamental idea of freedom is not affected by the accidents of time and circumstance. It does not vary with the centuries, nor with the comings and goings of men or empires. The substance of Truth does not change, nor does the substance of freedom'

Pádraig Pearse

KILMICHAEL

by 'Eyewitness'

This article dealing with the attack by the West Cork Brigade flying column of the Irish Republican Army on British forces on 28 November 1920 at Kilmichael will not be presented in the same manner as was my article which dealt with the fight at Crossbarry. The latter article was constructed as a strategical and tactical study of the largest and most successful operation of the Anglo-Irish War. This cannot be so constructed because, although equally successful, the fight at Kilmichael was based on different and exceptional circumstances and although fierce and bloody it was of short duration. Within twenty minutes, the eighteen Auxiliaries were wiped out and there were no troop movements except one by the IRA during the stand-up fight. Hence it is written as a descriptive article rather than a strictly military study. This of course is not to suggest that conclusions cannot be drawn from the story of this fight of at least equal importance to those drawn from the study of Crossbarry.

Needs of the Time

Such actions as that fought out at Kilmichael do not normally take place between opposing armies. This fight was born of the needs of that time of travail and it is essential to a study of the battle not alone to deal with movements, dispositions, terrain and the action itself but to present clearly all the circumstances which led up to and prevailed at the time of the action. Without those, this article could easily be misinterpreted for the fight was not an orthodox military operation. If it were it would be easy to criticise the column commander for taking undue risks with his column, for his disposition of the column in action, for his selection of terrain, and for putting to too great a test untried and even untrained troops. Therefore judge this action against the terror the Auxiliaries had created, against the sorrows and sufferings of the Irish people and against the death and destruction they had to face. Feel, as the Volunteer leaders did, the paramount importance of stopping the terror and stopping it decisively for now the stake was no longer only that of continuing armed resistance against the foreigner but of saving the citizens from humiliations, attacks and death itself. Judge it too not only in its bitterness and hates but also in its higher plane for all good Volunteers then felt that the spirit of those who had suffered and died for Ireland throughout the ages would inspire them in their effort to smash these savage mercenaries who had the name of being super fighters. Above all judge it clearly understanding that the fight was planned and carried out on the basis that the IRA would be well satisfied to lose man for man in smashing the Auxiliaries, for the nation's morale could not for long be maintained were its citizens to be killed off without an armed challenge. And although many units had been preparing, the honour of first meeting the Auxiliaries in arms fell to the West Cork Brigade flying column.

The Auxiliaries

Of all the ruthless forces that occupied Ireland down the centuries, the Auxiliaries were surely the worst. They were recruited early in 1920 from ex-British officers who had held commissioned rank and had had active service in one or more of the theatres of the Great War. They were openly established as a terrorist body with the avowed object of breaking by force Ireland's continuing resistance to British rule. Their war ranks ranged from lieutenant to brigadier-general and they were assumed to be the very pick of Britain's best fighters. Highly paid, they even dressed in a special uniform calculated to cow their opponents. Each carried a rifle, two revolvers, one strapped to each thigh, and two Mills bombs.[*]

This then was the force that the West Cork flying column prepared to meet. Unfortunately the fact that the Auxiliaries had up to then been immune from attack and allowed to smash and bluster their way through the country without armed challenge had had a bad effect on national morale. Whispers were current that the 'Auxies' were super-fighters and all but invincible. There could be no further delay in challenging them.

Here it is only fair to say that the better type of British officer did not join them and that those who did quickly resigned when they found out the general type of its members and the nature of the work they were expected to do. Amongst those who left was the first commanding officer, Brigadier-General Crozier. He wrote a book *Ireland for Ever* and in it he throws some light on the cruelties and indiscipline of the Auxiliary force. It should also be stated that on many occasions British army officers and men interfered to prevent beatings and killings of Irish citizens by the 'Auxies'.

The Column

The West Cork column which had fought at Toureen, Bandon and part of which had fought at Newcestown was composed of

---

[*] *Author's Note*: Owing to the international situation the author has directed that a paragraph be deleted from the article.

brigade, battalion and company officers. At the end of October they were returned to their units for area duties. The next column was mobilised on 22 November, and was composed entirely of new men except for the column commander and one other who had been with the previous column. None outside those two mentioned had been in action before and indeed only a few had ever fired a round out of a rifle even at target practice. The column strength was the commander and thirty others. Six other men should have mobilised but owing to a mistake they did not turn up until the day of the fight, when they were not alone too late but were very nearly the cause of disaster to the column. The column was divided into three sections each consisting of a section commander and nine men and training started near Togher, north-west of Dunmanway of 22 November. However, enemy activity interrupted the training and several moves had to be made so that on the day before the fight the flying column was camped sixteen miles south-east of Togher at Shanaway having had only about three days training. Owing to the shortage of ammunition only three rounds per man could be allowed for target practice.

The column mobilised at midnight on Saturday 27 November. Each man was armed with a rifle and only thirty-five rounds. A few had revolvers and the commander had also two Mills bombs. Untried and even untrained, they were fit, hard and above all had that high morale of Volunteers who knew that they were about to fight for that highest of causes – a people's freedom. They knew that there would not be a drawn battle with the Auxiliaries; they had either to win or be wiped out. At 1 a.m. they moved off and filed past that great Irish priest, Father (now canon) O'Connell, Enniskeane, who had come out to hear their Confessions. Through the night they marched by roads, by-roads and across country towards the position which had been selected the previous day. And as they walked silently through sleet and cold, many thoughts dwelt on the death and destruction, the havoc and humiliations inflicted on their people by the terrorists they were about to meet. Shortly after dawn broke, at 8.30 a.m., the flying column, after an eighteen miles march, reached the ambush position at Kilmichael.

Terrain

On the four successive Sundays preceding Sunday, 28 November 1920, two lorries loaded with Auxiliaries, estimated between eighteen and twenty in number, travelled from Macroom to Glan Cross, from which they diverged to either Coppeen, Castletown-Kenneigh, Manch or Dunmanway on raiding expeditions. Therefore the ambush position had to be selected at a point north of Glan Cross so as to ensure an action. The West Cork Brigade boundary ran west through Coppeen and on through Glan and this fact, in addition to the advisability of attacking the enemy as far away from his Macroom base as possible, necessitated the selection of a position south of Kilmichael Cross. The position chosen was one and a half miles south of Kilmichael Cross which is about one and a quarter miles north of the Glan Cross of three roads.

Here the road quarter-circles from the north in to the ambush position, from where it turns east for a distance of one hundred and seventy yards to the end of the action area, whence it travels south through Glan Cross on to Dunmanway. This one hundred and seventy yards stretch is broken by a bend about halfway, so that a person standing on the road at either end would only have a view of about one hundred yards of the road. There is a gradual fall in the road from the west and there are no ditches along that stretch. Branching off from the road at the western entrance to the position is an unprotected passageway leading to a farmhouse about one hundred and fifty yards to the south-west. At the other end, the eastern outlet, where the road turns south again there is a small field north-east of the road. It is protected by a stone wall running north to south alongside the road and another similar wall about two-and-a-half feet high of loose stones running north-west from the road. The angle where these two walls meet juts sharply on to the road making an ideal, if sparsely protected, enfilade position facing westwards.

Around the ambush area the bleak and barren countryside is bogland interspersed with the heather-covered rocky eminences. North of the road, at the western entrance bend, rises one such rocky eminence about nine feet high at the very edge of the road. It extends at varying heights northwards for about seventy yards. East of this height the ground is boggy and low-lying for about one hundred and forty yards when another rocky hillock is encountered. This also is about nine feet high and extends along the road edge for about twenty-five yards to within yards of the enfilading position. Travelling again eastwards about sixty yards from the entrance bend on the southern side of the road there is a fairly large rock. Fifteen yards further on, also on the edge of the road, is a smaller rock. South of these two rocks the land is boggy for a depth of fifty yards until it meets a chain of rocks which runs parallel to the one hundred and seventy yards stretch of road.

Dispositions

Before the Volunteers of the flying column were posted to their action positions, they were paraded by the column commander who gave them the following orders:

1. There was to be no retreat from the ambush positions until victory had been won. The fight could only end either in the decisive smashing of the Auxiliaries or the smashing

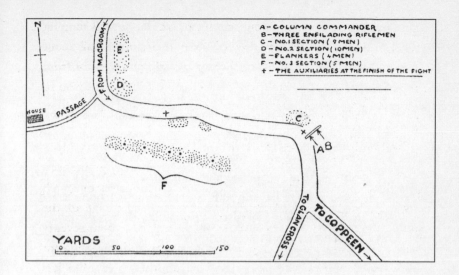

of the column and it had to be fought out to the finish. Consequently there was no plan for a retirement until the column marched away back the road after victory.

2. Once the enemy approach was signalled, no Volunteer was in any circumstances to show himself until the attack was opened. The first lorry was to be allowed to come through the position to within fifty yards of the command post when a bomb would be thrown and the whistle blown as the signal for a general attack. The various sections were to concentrate their fire on the primary targets allotted to them and if any of the sections or sub-sections were unable to see the enemy, on no account were they to leave their positions to seek the Auxiliaries because of the danger of leaving uncovered any part of the road.

3. No. 1 section of nine riflemen was to occupy the large rocky eminence at the eastern outlet of the ambush position. From here they were able to fire on to any part of the one hundred and seventy yards stretch of the stretch of

road and its adjoining terrain, except the ground and road immediately under their position. Their primary target was to be the occupants of the first lorry.

4. No. 2 section was to occupy the large rock on the roadside at the western entrance bend. This section, which was strengthened by the arrival after the column of an officer armed with a rifle, numbered ten men. Because of its position at an actual bend of the road, seven men were posted so as to be able to fire on any enemy who rounded the entrance bend, whilst the remaining three were placed so that they could attack any who had not reached that point. The primary target of this section was to be the occupants of the second lorry.

5. A sub-section of four riflemen from No. 3 section were to occupy the high rocky ground sixty yards north of No. 2 section. From this position, where they covered about two hundred and fifty yards of the approach road, they were to attack any enemy lorries other than first two.

6. The remaining five riflemen of No. 3 section including the section commander were to occupy the chain of rocks south of the road. Their primary duty was to prevent the Auxiliaries from securing any of the high ground on their side of the road.

7. Three riflemen were to occupy the enfilade position close to No. 1 section. Their primary target was of course to be the first oncoming lorry.

8. The command post was to be a few yards from the enfilading riflemen.

9. Two unarmed scouts were posted one hundred and fifty and two hundred yards north of No. 2 section from where

they were in a position to signal the enemy approach nearly a mile distant. A third unarmed scout was placed one hundred and fifty yards to the south of the command post to prevent surprise by the enemy from that direction.

The positions were occupied by 9 a.m. The column had no food with them and although a friendly house sent on all its available food and a bucket of tea, there was not enough for the whole column. As the hours passed the Volunteers suffered from the intense cold as they lay waiting for the enemy. Towards evening the gloom deepened over that bleak Kilmichael countryside.

KILMICHAEL
– PART II

by 'Eyewitness'

The action

At 4.5 p.m. [*sic*] the distant scout signalled the approach of the enemy. At that very moment around the entrance bend came a sidecar with five Volunteers on it fully equipped and carrying their rifles in their hands. Those were the men who should have joined the column on the previous Monday. They had reached the passageway when the column commander shouted 'Get them off the road. Gallop up the passageway. The Auxies are here. Keep galloping.' In thirty seconds they had galloped out of sight. Thirty seconds later at a fast pace the first lorry of Auxiliaries sailed around the bend into the ambush position.

On reaching the half-way bend the occupants of the first lorry must have immediately seen the armed Volunteer officer in uniform facing them one hundred yards on. Yet, as was anticipated, the driver did not apply his brakes until he had travelled a further fifty yards. At this point a bomb was thrown, the whistle blew and a volley rang out. The bomb soared through the air to meet the oncoming lorry and luckily landed in the driver's seat, where it exploded almost at contact. The lorry lurched drunkenly out of control but still came on, impelled by its own weight and with the foot brake released by the dead driver. On it came with some of the Auxiliaries firing with revolvers and the IRA pouring revolver and rifle fire into it at point-blank range as it came to rest within a few feet of the small stone wall manned by the column commander and three others.[*]

Meanwhile the second lorry which was travelling one hundred and fifty yards behind the first had followed into the ambuscade. It was directed opposite No. 2 section when the attack was opened on the first lorry. No. 2 section opened fire on it and although they must have hit a few, all the Auxiliaries were able to jump out when the lorry was halted thirty yards further on. The Auxiliaries of this lorry threw themselves on the roadside facing No. 2 section and opened rifle fire on them at once. The Auxiliaries were deployed with the large rocky hillock on the eastern edge of the road effectively protecting some of them from the fire of No. 3 section. The fighting between the second lot of Auxiliaries and No. 2 section continued for about five minutes by which time Battalion Vice-Commandant Michael McCarthy and at least one Auxiliary were killed.

By this time the first lorry had been wiped out and the column commander now brought out the three riflemen from the enfilading position on the road to attack the second lot of Auxiliaries from the rear. The four ran crouching up the road towards where the fight was being waged. They had only gone about twenty yards when they were surprised to hear the firing stop and a number of Auxiliaries chant 'We surrender' as they grounded their rifles. Quickly four Volunteers of No. 2 section stood up to take the surrender but quicker still the Auxiliaries opened fire on them with revolvers mortally wounding Lieutenant Pat Deasy, Kilmacsimon Quay, and killing outright Lieutenant Jim O'Sullivan of Rossmore.

---

[*] *Author's Note*: Owing to the international situation the author has directed that a paragraph be deleted from the article.

While this tragedy was being enacted in the amazingly short time between the bogus surrender and the treacherous shooting of Deasy and O'Sullivan, the column commander and the three riflemen continued to move up to the enemy. As their comrades fell they completed a rush which brought them within thirty yards of the Auxiliaries. They opened fire at once. The position now was that of the seven riflemen of No. 2 section who were in a position to fire on the enemy only four remained. Those gallantly kept the fight going and continued to fire on the Auxiliaries who were firing from a lying position on the road, once again using rifles. Thirty yards behind the Auxiliaries, also lying on the road were the reinforcing IRA party who poured lead into them from a range from which they could not very well miss. Sandwiched between the two small parties of the IRA, who numbered eight in all, the survivors of this party of nine Auxiliaries were soon smashed. Eight were dead and the one survivor died some hours afterwards from wounds. The fight at Kilmichael was over.

The Retirement

The column was ordered out on the road and guards were posted. Lieutenant Deasy who was only fifteen years and nine months was bandaged. He was dying. A door was procured and he was borne away some miles by scouts to a friendly house where he died some hours later. The bodies of Vice-Commandant MacCarthy and Lieutenant O'Sullivan were relieved of their equipment and reverently laid on the heather covered rock on which they had fallen and a scout sent off to arrange for their removal. Eighteen rifles, thirty revolvers, ammunition, Mills bombs, notebooks and papers useful to the IRA intelligence department were collected. Then when the bodies of the Auxiliaries were removed from the vicinity the lorries were set on fire.

It was now dark but the blaze of the burning lorries lit up the corpse-strewn road and bleak countryside as the flying column paraded: the order 'Present Arms' was given. After this final salute, advance and rearguards were detailed and the column marched away to the south in search of comparative safety across the Bandon river. Through the night they marched carrying the captured equipment and arms. Drenched by the wind-driven rain from the south they passed through Shanacashel, Coolnagow, Balteenbrack and across the Bandon river at Manch Bridge. Still on to the south until they reached Granure where they halted at an unoccupied labourer's cottage.

Here the local Volunteers put out a chain of scouts after which they supplied food to the column. Then from neighbours' ricks they brought bundles of straw to the cottage and enabled the weary flying column to rest. This flying column, in a period of twenty-four hours, marched thirty-six miles in rough going, lay cramped and half-frozen on the damp ground without being able to risk enough movement to warm themselves for seven hours and fought a successful and desperate action. And further, throughout that period many of them had no food whatever.

Commentary and Conclusions

Some of the lessons of the fight at Kilmichael detailed hereunder require a commentary to ensure the deduction of true conclusions. They are as follows:

1. The situation prevailing in November 1920, fully justified the IRA column policy to attack without delay those Auxiliaries even at the cost of losing man for man in any action. It were far better that Volunteers should die fighting and killing off at least some of the enemy than to be killed off without hitting back.

2. The column commander is open to criticism for not mobilising the column earlier and allowing it a further week's training.

3. The ambush position selected was the best of the bad lot available between Kilmichael and Gleann (Glan) Cross. To ensure the fight and to keep near the West Cork Brigade area at a reasonably safe distance from the enemy garrison at Macroom, the column was limited to this stretch of roadway.

4. The column commander is open to criticism because he did not arrange for food for his column. Sandwiches could easily have been carried. Furthermore in view of the probable ordeal before his column it would have been better if he had marched the column to within three or four miles of the ambush position on Friday night so that the men would have been fresh for action and have had some sleep.

5. The protection arrangements for the column were weak. There was no reserve for the column and the column commander undoubtedly, but quite aware of the dangers, took a risk in allocating only four riflemen to the task of firing on and holding up any enemy lorries other than the two which were to be allowed into the ambuscade. But where were the reserve or the additional strength for this flanking party to come from? They could only be obtained by reducing the main striking power which was already in effect only twenty riflemen – the expected enemy strength. Any further reduction of the striking force which was certain to be required, for the formation of a reserve or the strengthening of a flank which was NOT certain to be required, would not have been justified.

6. The action stations of all three sections were satisfactory as the ensuing fight proved. Generally speaking the placing of a section across the road from the main attacking sections is not advisable. Owing to the terrain it was not alone advisable here, but absolutely necessary in order to prevent the Auxiliaries from reaching the hillocks occupied by No. 3 section. This a number of the Auxiliaries might easily have done as there was no ditch to cross had not No. 3 section already occupied them. Indeed No. 3 section did splendid work under its competent section commander.

7. The enfilading position at the southern and of the ambush which was manned by three riflemen was a main contributing factor to the success of the column. It was only some loose stones built without any binding to a height of a few feet. From it those three riflemen were able to fire direct on to the oncoming lorry, fight well at close quarters and eventually go to the aid of their hard-pressed comrades of No. 2 section. Too much stress cannot be laid on the importance of enfilade fire in any action.

8. The fortunes of war were certainly with the IRA in the action. Had the Auxiliaries arrived thirty seconds earlier, they would have opened the fight by attacking the sidecar of late-arriving Volunteers at the entrance to the ambush position, it is idle to speculate how the eventful fight would have turned out although an interesting exercise might be worked out by officers on the assumption that this occurred and that they were acting as the IRA column commander. Alternatively, a second problem might be worked out by officers assuming that they were in the position of Lieutenant-Colonel Craik who commanded the Auxiliaries at Kilmichael.

9. The IRA tactics of surprise, close-quarter attack and the maintaining of every possible man as part of the striking force even at some risk to the protection of the column succeeded.

10. Only Volunteers who were physically very fit could have stood the test of endurance from the mobilisation at Shanaway to their arrival at the unoccupied cottage at Granure twenty-five hours later.

Finally, perhaps the main reason for the IRA success at Kilmichael was that the column marched into position as fighters, seeking fight. Knowing only too well their own limitations in numbers, training and armament, fully aware of the reputed prowess and savagery of the Auxiliaries, they sought out the invading terrorists. And at that spot, now marked with a simple iron cross, where MacCarthy, Deasy and O'Sullivan fell, they smashed forever the power of that evil force.

A FIGHT IN CLARE IN 1920:
THE STORY OF THE RINEEN AMBUSH

by Sergeant J.J. Neylon, Infantry Corps

In September 1920, the Mid-Clare Brigade had so far perfected their organisation in training, arming, and discipline that it was felt that they as a brigade were competent to carry the fight to the enemy and attack his convoys and scouting parties with a reasonable hope of success. In the fourth battalion, of which I was commanding officer, we felt that we should justify ourselves as a unit of the brigade. In looking round our area for a suitable attack objective we found that a lorry of RIC and Black and Tans was accustomed to travel from Ennistymon to Miltown-Malbay every Wednesday at 10.30 a.m., returning at 12.30 p.m. Having confirmed our intelligence reports on these movements, we felt fairly certain that we could establish contact on any Wednesday we chose. The 22 September was decided on finally, and early on that morning the column moved into position at Rineen Cross, halfway between Lahinch and Miltown-Malbay.

Terrain

The ambush locale might be described as 'Rolling Country' – with low hills and hollows and a fairly steep falling gradient on the road from Miltown to Rineen Cross. The hillocks which commanded all roads provided excellent observation posts. A good idea of the general configuration can be got from the map. Rineen was at a junction where a by-road left the Lahinch-Miltown road and slanted south-west across the West Clare Railway, which paralleled the main road about forty yards south. South of the railway was mainly bogland, and about a quarter mile north was the sea.

Disposition

Our party was divided into three sections, with scouts posted on the hill marked 'A', commanding the main road in both directions. The main force, forty strong, was placed between the railway and

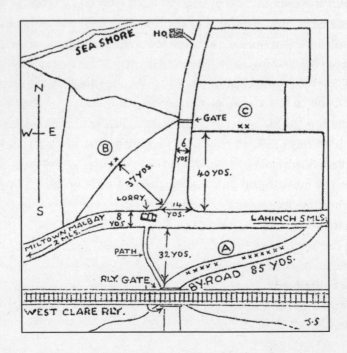

the road west of the Cross, at a range of thirty yards. This section was to deliver the main attack, and shall be called section I. Section II, of five riflemen, seven with shot-guns, and two with hand-grenades, was posted on the right flank of section I with orders to shoot the lorry driver, thereby stopping the lorry where it could be best engaged by section I. Section III was on the opposite side of the road from section I, and would combine with them in concentrating fire from both sides on the lorry when it had been stopped. Ferns and furze bushes were collected and 'planted' in the fences in front of us, affording complete concealment. The stage was set.

The Engagement

On the approach of the out-going convoy in the morning, our scouts inaccurately reported three lorries, and as our position was prepared to deal with only one, it was decided to postpone the attack until the return journey, when fresh dispositions of our forces could be made. On discovering that in fact there was only one lorry, we remained in the old positions and awaited its return.

At about 12.30 p.m., our scouts signalled – correctly this time – the approach of one lorry from Miltown. The men, although most of them had not previously been in action, waited steadily and confidently for the signal to open up, which as arranged, was given by me firing on the lorry. Section II, under Ignatius O'Neill, opened fire immediately, accounting for driver with their first burst.

The lorry now ran into the ditch, where sections I and III engaged its crew, and in a few minutes the fight was over and won. The entire personnel of the enemy – seven men – were killed. We captured six rifles, a service revolver, 3,000 rounds of .303 and fifty rounds of .45 ammunition.

Surprised

However, the day's work was not over. Just as we had collected the captured equipment, our scouts signalled the approach of enemy army lorries in force. This party, we afterwards learned, knew nothing of our engagement, but had been called out to the West Clare area, about fifteen miles beyond our position, where another column had been active that day and a resident magistrate had been killed.

The enemy had ten or twelve lorries, with upwards of one hundred and fifty men. As we had been taken unawares, away from our original ambush positions, they would inevitably discover us, and it became obvious that we must fight a rearguard action to save ourselves and our equipment. They lost no time in dismounting, deploying, and taking up positions for attack. We prepared equally rapidly to resist them. They attacked with three machine guns and rifle fire. Our main body broke up into sections and retreated south, the men conducting themselves like veterans, taking advantage of every ditch, drain and watercourse, and firing with cool steadiness while machine-gun bursts were scything the grass around them. Once across the railway we took to the bogs beyond it – a very difficult type of country for the military, who did not know the terrain, to follow us over. Section III retreated north to the sea and dispersed without being seriously engaged. Ignatius O'Neill directed the rearguard action, which was fought in its early stages in the classic style – one section retiring while the other section covered them. Once the bogland was reached the men split into small groups and, firing just often enough to keep the enemy well back, scattered to their hiding places. Firing ceased at about 2,000 yards. In this part of the engagement four of our men sustained minor wounds. Enemy casualties were afterwards assessed at fourteen killed. That night, many buildings in Ennistymon, Lahinch, and Miltown Malbay were burned as reprisals.

The rearguard action lasted about three hours, but the spoils of the ambush were worth it. Indeed, we could not have fought the second convoy at all without these, as our ammunition stocks were very low.

The captured arms and ammunitions were of incalculable value to our hitherto weakly-equipped column, and were afterwards employed in the engagements at Monreal and Ruan, and in many other major activities of the Mid-Clare column.

Commentary on the Ambush
by Colonel F.J. Henry

Positions

Section II was ideally placed, on the only good ambush site along the seven miles from Lahinch to Miltown-Malbay. It afforded good cover as evidenced by the fact that the lorry passed through on the first journey without suspicion. Its cover value was certainly much enhanced by ingenious camouflaging with furze and ferns.

The other positions were not so well sited, and, although they afforded cover in action they were in danger of exposure to fire from their own outposts. Withdrawals from these positions entailed exposure.

Observation

A salutary lesson was learned on the importance of good scouting and the necessity of guarding against surprise. Had it not been for the scouts' vigilance the success of the first ambush might have been turned into a calamitous rout by the unexpected arrival of the second enemy force. Against this, in the morning inaccurate information was passed back which might have meant the failure of the entire plan, and the scouts seem either to have delayed culpably in transmitting information of the arrival of the second military convoy, or to have failed to observe it until it was almost on top of the column.

Grenades

The grenades, when thrown, did not explode on the road, but in the field on the opposite side. They were obviously thrown in the regulation way, falling beyond the target because of the short distance, and it would, therefore, have been more effective to roll or lob them into the road.

Fire-Discipline

The fire-discipline of the column must have been excellent, when one remembers that the men, with little or no active service training, waited coolly and withheld their fire until the lorry was only thirty yards away. This contrasts very notably with some other ambushes, where over-enthusiasm or carelessness allowed fire to be opened too early, betraying the positions and jeopardising the success of the engagements.

CAPTURE OF RUAN RIC BARRACKS:
MID-CLARE BRIGADE EXPLOIT OF 1920

by Commandant J. Barrett

Ruan RIC barrack was strategically situated. Commanding one of the approaches to Ennis, it was a pivotal point in the British chain of defences. At a convenient junction in the centre of Mid-Clare Brigade, it was a useful eye in the enemy's intelligence machine. The brigade staff was quick to recognise the benefits reaped by the enemy from the maintenance of this stronghold. They found, too, by experience, that it was a thorn in their own side as its particular position hampered the free movement of brigade and battalion officers.

The brigade staff decided to attack the barrack with a view to its capture or the consequent withdrawal of its garrison by the authorities. This was a formidable task. Well-built, strongly fortified, fitted with steel shutters and sandbags, and encircled with a barbed wire, Ruan would seem to be impregnable to all forms of attack without the aid of artillery. There was no artillery available. Nevertheless the staff was undaunted. The place must be reduced!

Intelligence Officers find Heel of Achilles

After patient concentration it was discovered that this seemingly impregnable fortress had its weak point, after all. It became known to our intelligence that a constable used to leave the barrack every morning for milk between the hours of seven and eight. The house in which he got the milk stood at the rear of the barracks, at a distance of some three hundred and four hundred yards. Making his exit by the back door, the constable followed a pathway between the out-offices and the boundary wall. The wall was roughly seven feet high. The pathway, six feet wide, was obstructed by barbed wire entanglements some five feet high. On the outward journey the constable used to push aside portion of the entanglement and leave it in position until his return. Here was the key to attack – the heel of Achilles! On receipt of this information it was agreed that the attack should be made in the morning, and that it should be made to centre round the back entrance. Further reconnaissance revealed some minor difficulties within the grounds and in the vicinity. The paved pathway was heard to resound to the tramp of shod feet; the dogs in the neighbourhood, by loud and prolonged barking signalled the slightest movement at night. For the first of these there was an obvious solution; for the second, one was forthcoming.

System of Road Obstructions

A most formidable danger still remained – the danger of being discovered and hemmed in by superior forces from Ennis in the course of the attack. To obviate this serious difficulty an elaborate and widespread system of road obstruction was made an integral part of the attack. Two rings of obstructions were considered necessary. One, the inner one, blocked all approaches to the immediate vicinity of the barrack; the other harassed advance along the remote parts of roads leading to Ruan. The inner ring of obstruction was strong. It consisted of felled trees and hundreds of tons of large stones. Each barricade, moreover was defended by a section leader and eight men armed with shot-guns. The outer ring was far-flung, and consisted of some twenty barricades scattered along all roads radiating from Ruan, extending at times to a distance of ten miles. This network of obstructions was allotted to the 3rd Battalion, assisted by two companies from the 1st and two companies from the 5th Battalions.

Attacking Party and the Lay-Out of their Objective

The barrack was a three-storeyed building, garrisoned by two sergeants and eleven men. The ground floor comprised a kitchen, dining-room, hall, pantry and bedroom. Upstairs, there were three bedrooms. In the absence of a plan it will be found helpful to number the apartments No. 1: kitchen, where two constables armed with rifles and revolvers kept guard; No. 2: sergeant's bedroom; No. 3: dining-room; No. 4: hall; No. 5: pantry – all on the ground floor. No. 6: large bedroom to accommodate six men; No. 7: medium bedroom to accommodate three men; No. 8: sergeant's bedroom – upstairs. Two officers and five section leaders with twenty-nine men were detailed to deal with every apartment of the building: one officer and four men for the kitchen; a section leader and two men for the sergeant's room (No. 2); a section leader and seven men for the large bedroom upstairs (No. 6); a section leader and four men for the medium bedroom (No. 7); a section leader and two men for sergeant's room (No. 8); a section leader and two men to detain the milkman; and finally, an officer and three men to reinforce or cover the retreat of those entering the room as the circumstances demanded.

Men, picked for coolness, dash and courage, and drawn from all areas of the brigade, were set aside for the immediate work of storming the barrack. They were divided into two sections: the

117

attacking party proper, and the covering party. The attacking party consisted of two officers and twenty-nine men; the covering party of three officers and twenty-one men.

Mobilisation

On the evening of the attack the picked men foregathered at various centres, some distance from Ruan. At nightfall they were mobilised in a vacant house about four miles from the barrack. Each section was allotted its special task. The nature of the operation was explained, and far from deterring the men, the delicacy of the job filled them with added enthusiasm and eagerness. In the early hours of morning of 14 October, under cover of darkness, the raiders moved in the direction of the barrack. The covering party was guided to its position by ten scouts and five guides. This party was divided into three sections, each section consisting of one officer and seven men. These three groups occupied the best available positions in the vicinity of the barrack. Their duty was to deal with any of the reinforcements that might evade the obstruction parties, and to cover the retreat of the attacking party proper.

In a wood, about half a mile from their objective, the attacking party removed their boots and marched barefoot to the high wall at the rear of the barrack. Fortunately there was no comment by the dogs of the neighbourhood. The poison had done its work! Each section leader held his men in readiness for the order to march.

The Assault

At approximately 7.30 a.m. the RIC man was heard leaving the barrack for milk; a few minutes later the signal was given for the assault. All sections moved according to plan; the guard was disarmed; each apartment was approached by its allotted group; and the small covering party took up position with clock-like precision. The police were disarmed, and surrendered without resistance, except those in No. 6, the large bedroom upstairs. In an exchange of shots which took place here between the assailants and the RIC, three RIC men were wounded, one fatally. When the surrender was complete our men rendered first-aid, and hastened to procure a priest and a doctor. No time was lost; the arms, bicycles, ammunition and other equipment were moved to a waiting char-á-banc, which moved off with an escort to a pre-arranged destination. The wounded constables, having received spiritual and medical attention, were taken to houses in the neighbourhood where they received continued assistance. In the meantime the RIC men were being exercised in foot-drill while our men were busy preparing the barracks for demolition. When the demolition was complete the RIC men were conducted to some houses in the vicinity. They were provided with breakfast and warned not to leave these houses for at least one hour. They gave an undertaking – under some pressure – not to countenance, encourage, or take part in local burnings or reprisals of any kind. Local unionists were warned, moreover, that if crown forces carried out any reprisals in the vicinity, their mansions, now upgraded, would suffer in consequence. These warnings had the desired effect.

Booty

The booty consisted of thirteen bicycles, fifteen rifles, fourteen revolvers, one automatic pistol, two Verey light pistols, two shotguns; 1,000 rounds of .303 ammunition, seven hundred rounds of .45 ammunition, fifty rounds of automatic ammunition, two hundred rounds of buckshot ammunition, three boxes of hand grenades, one case of rifle-grenades, some Verey light cartridges and a box of assorted ammunition. This fine haul helped the brigade to equip a comparatively strong active service unit. The captors were justly proud of their work, which they had carried out with utmost efficiency. Elated and encouraged, they returned to their respective areas.

THE FIGHT AT ASHBOURNE:
A STIRRING EPISODE OF THE 1916 RISING

by Major J.V. Lawless, Cavalry Corps

This stirring episode of the 1916 Rising may not be as familiar to readers as the fighting in the city, with its more spectacular destruction of buildings. The fight at Ashbourne may also be found useful as illustrating the value in minor military operations of such vital factors as morale, discipline, tactical training, leadership, surprise and protection.

The Fingal Volunteers

It is interesting to remember that the Fingal Volunteers in 1916 were in fact the prototype of our present-day cyclist squadrons, and although the significance of their existence as a cavalry unit was not understood or recognised even by themselves, they did in fact, to a great extent, adopt correct cavalry tactics in the series of raids and reconnaissance movements carried out throughout North County Dublin from Easter Monday till the Friday of that week, when the first really serious engagement took place at Ashbourne, County Meath, just over the county boundary.

Previous to Ashbourne, the column, about forty-five strong, all mounted on bicycles, had been engaged during the week in a series of lightning raids upon RIC barracks and communications in the area, with the threefold purpose of collecting some much-needed arms, hampering enemy movements and drawing some enemy attentions away from the hard-pressed Volunteers fighting in the city. Originally we had had twenty more men, but this number had, on orders from James Connolly, been sent in to the city from our camp at Finglas. These twenty gave a good account of themselves in the fighting in O'Connell Street, and at the Mendicity Institute, where one of their number was killed.

It may be well, before proceeding to the description of the actual fight, to give some kind of picture of the organisation and equipment of the Volunteer unit, so that the reader may more readily grasp the significance of later details.

The Volunteers of North County Dublin or Fingal, as the territory is known, constituted, up to 1916, the 5th Battalion of the Dublin Brigade, but like most Volunteer units of the time was never near battalion strength. In fact, if memory serves me right, I think the area at that period was, at best, able to muster a strength of about only one infantry company. Due, however, among other causes, to the confusion of cancelled orders on Easter Sunday, little more than half the number answered the mobilisation call.

The following summary of the equipment of the Fingal Volunteers on Easter Monday is taken from some old notes of mine:

Arms

Modern Service Rifles including long and short Lee-Enfield and 9 m/m Mauser – 12 to 15. Old type Mauser (Howth rifle) – 10 to 12.

Martini Enfield Single Shot Carbine – 12 to 15.

Single barrel 12 bore shot-guns – 20 to 30.

Revolvers and pistols, various types and calibres (.455, .38, .32, .25) – 12 to 14.

Ammunition: total available in the unit

303 and 9 m/m – About one hundred rounds per weapon.
Old Mauser – About sixty rounds per weapon.
Shot-gun loaded with buckshot – About three hundred rounds per weapon.
Pistol ammunition, various – About thirty rounds per weapon.

Uniform and Equipment

About fifteen to twenty, including most of the officers, had uniforms. The remainder wore their equipment – bandolier, haversack and belt – over their civilian clothes.

Bicycles

Most of the men who reported on Easter Monday did so on bicycles.

Transport

One horse and a farm draw belonging to my father was the only heavy transport until the commandeering on Wednesday of a Ford motor bread-van. In addition to this, there was a Morris-Oxford two-seater belonging to Doctor Hayes, and a motor-cycle belonging to Thomas Ashe.

Explosives

Sixty pounds gelignite which was used to destroy the GNR line on Easter Monday. There remained two home-made canister grenades.

On the arrival in camp of five or six stragglers from city units and the detachment on Tuesday from our camp at Finglas of twenty men to the city, the urgent need for a reorganisation of our force arose. We had received orders from James Connolly at the GPO that our activities were to take the form of diverting enemy attention and troops, if possible, from the city, and a rapid survey of the situation resulted in throwing overboard the old British infantry organisation, upon which we had been trained, and the adoption of a scheme made to fit the numbers available and the tactical requirements of our mission.

The arrangement adopted, which incidentally was quite sound from a cavalry viewpoint, was to divide the entire force into four more or less equal sections of ten to twelve men, each section under command of an officer, the remaining four senior officers constituting the headquarters and command staff.

The operation procedure adopted was that each day one section was detailed for foraging duty with the job of protecting the camp day and night, and also locating and procuring food supplies for the column. The remaining three sections, proceeding on the daily raid or other mission, moved always with the sections so spaced and detailed that the leading section constituted the advance guard; the rearmost section the rearguard, while the commanding officer with his staff moved normally with the main body, in between. The sections changed over duties daily.

Ashe and Mulcahy

The commander and the staff of the column were largely, if not entirely, responsible for the success of the unit. Thomas Ashe, the commander, was a fine physical specimen of manhood, courageous, and high principled; something of a poet, painter and dreamer, in military matters he was, perhaps, somewhat unpractical. Early in the week, however, we had been joined by a few stragglers from a city battalion, amongst whom was Dick Mulcahy. Mulcahy was known already to the other members of the staff, and it was soon apparent to everyone that his was the mind necessary to plan and direct operations. Cool, clear-headed and practical, and with a personality and tact that enabled him to take virtual control of the situation, without in any way undermining Ashe's prestige as a commander. My father, Frank Lawless, was a quartermaster, and because of his wide local knowledge of the country and the four people was of great help in planning operations and movements, as well as in the essential matter of supplies. Dr Dick Hayes, the other member of the staff, in addition to his medical duties, was a valuable voice in the staff councils, and was also available for intelligence duties.

To come, however, to the engagement at Ashbourne we must skip the other incidents from the mobilisation on Easter Monday to the morning of Friday of that week.

The column had bivouacked late on Thursday night at a derelict farmhouse at Borranstown, about three miles south of Garristown. Information had come in that considerable bodies of troops were preparing to move from Athlone to Dublin per Midland Great Western Railway, so it was decided to cut the railway line, and thereafter to harass the troops who might arrive at the breach in the line. With this object in view the column left the bivouac area between 10 and 11 o'clock on Friday morning, the immediate objective being the Midland Great Western Railway line at Batterstown, about twelve miles away.

The Attack on the Barracks

As the column moved out that Friday morning it occurred to someone that the Ashbourne RIC Barracks, which was on our route, might not have evacuated, as others had been as the result

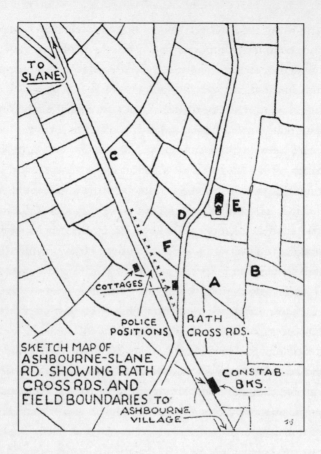

SKETCH MAP OF ASHBOURNE-SLANE RD. SHOWING RATH CROSS RDS. AND FIELD BOUNDARIES

of our raids. Scouts sent out returned with word that barracks was in a state of defence, and that a barricade was in course of erection across the main road in front of the barracks. The advance guard, therefore, moved carefully forward; the two men forming the point of the advance guard challenged and, after a slight scuffle, captured and disarmed the two RIC men who were working upon the barricade; the prisoners being marched to the rear, where they remained under guard. The remainder of the advance-guard section, leaving their bicycles stacked on the by-road north of the crossroads, took up a position along the ditch south of the main road and in front of the barracks, while Ashe, climbing up on to the road, completely exposed, called on the police to surrender. They replied by firing on him though fortunately without effect. Up to this time the other two sections (the fourth section having remained in camp at Borranstown) had remained halted on the by-road about three or four hundred yards north of the cross-roads, and were unaware of what was happening when the firing started.

About this time instructions were received from Ashe that the 2nd and 3rd sections were to take cover along the ditches facing the rear of the barracks, and await further orders. Accordingly these two sections, (one of which was at my own command), moved into the ditch shown at 'A' on the accompanying sketch, having stacked their bicycles on the road adjoining. It was observed that the barracks had no windows facing north, so there was no purpose opening fire at a range of less than a hundred yards. The police inside were replying to the fire through the loopholes of the iron-shuttered windows, and for about half-an-hour showed no sign of capitulating, though it was afterwards evident that their morale was considerably shaken from the first burst of fire. An attempt was then made to throw one of our two home-made grenades at the barracks in the hope of breaking the door, which though splintered by bullets still held firm. The grenade, however, fell short of its objective and exploded in the garden in front, doing no damage, but the noise of the explosion was apparently all that was needed to finally break down the resistance; for shortly afterwards a white flag or handkerchief fluttered from a window.

A New Factor

Before, however, the beleaguered garrison had time to march out and hand up their arms, a new factor entered the situation, which encouraged them to change their minds and continue their resistance. This was the arrival of some twenty-four motor cars laden with police reinforcements.

It will be remembered that sections two and three were still in position 'A', and not having received any further instructions, were more or less in dark as to what was going on. The country around is quite flat, and high banks and thick hedges prevent any extended view beyond the length of a field, except along the main road. The first indication that something unforeseen had happened was when a heavy burst of fire, some of which passed in our direction, was heard from the north-west side of the crossroads. Going towards the crossroads to investigate, I met two Volunteers belonging to No. 1 section running along the ditch towards me. Their story was that they had been detailed to watch the main road north-west of the Cross, but becoming more interested in what was going on at the barracks behind them, they never noticed the arrival of the police reinforcements until the first car was within fifty yards of the crossroads. They then fired their rifles at the leading car, and, one of the rifles jamming (a Martini Carbine), they fled towards us to inform us that 'hundreds of police had arrived.' Actually, the number was about sixty to seventy, with three officers: one county inspector and two district inspectors.

The situation was definitely serious, the surprise of our force being complete, and (presumably) superior enemy forces in close contact. Knowing that Ashe and Mulcahy, who were with No. 1 section in front of the barracks, would by now know as much, or more, of the situation than we did, the two sections moved into the ditch at 'B' facing west, and prepared to abandon the bicycles and to fight a retiring action eastwards. A runner having failed to get in touch with No. 1 section on the south-east side of the barracks, I than went on this mission myself, leaving the No. 2 section commander in charge.

Leadership

I had not got very far when I noticed Mulcahy, evidently looking for us at about the original position we had just left at 'A'. He signalled us to advance to the by-road where our bicycles lay, and headed in the direction himself. Stray bullets were falling in the intervening ploughed field, but the example of Mulcahy walking unscathed across it encouraged us to move across at the double, without seeking the shelter of the ditches.

At the by-road, after a hurried consultation with Ashe, Mulcahy assured us that the police had not a chance of success, and that we are going to rout or capture the entire force. His words inspired confidence and dispelled our previous doubts. He outlined briefly the plan of attack, summarising the situation as follows: the police had been unaware of our presence until surprised by the fire of the two men at the crossroads, followed by the immediate fire from the remainder of the section at the barracks. Jumping from the cars, which pulled up on the left of the road at intervals of ten to twenty yards, they sought what cover was available in their immediate vicinity, and mostly in the deep ditch along the north-east side of the main road, as far as the cars extended. Some few did in fact seek a fire position in the drain cuttings of the bank on the opposite side of the road, but these were all killed or wounded in the early stages of the fight.

The position then was that, though we had been surprised by their unexpected arrival, the police were equally surprised by our presence there; but whereas we now had a fair idea of their numbers and position, they were quite in the dark concerning our position and strength.

Mulachy's Dispositions

Mulcahy first grasped this fact, and his plan of attack was to make full use of the morale factor by driving home a vigorous assault with all possible force, from the vicinity of the crossroads, and giving the enemy the impression of superior force on our side, by fire from the rear. He took the 3rd section, reinforced by half the men of No. 2 section, to support the main attack of No. 1 section from the crossroads, and Ashe led the remainder of No. 2 section, under cover of the hedge on the northern side of the road to the rear of the police position on the main road, which position would not be disclosed until the main attack was made, so as to cut off any attempt at enemy retreat. For this purpose one of the men carried the one remaining canister grenade, with the idea of blowing any car that tried to pass. The 4th section of our force, which had been left in camp that morning, had been sent for, but up to this time (about 1.30 p.m.) had not arrived.

Ashe returned to the main body, having posted us in position C (see map). This was the junction of a deep ditch bounding the north-east side of the main road, and a ditch running at right angles to it, the rearmost police car being seven hundred yards away in the direction of the crossroads.

Having noticed a motor-cycle standing on the opposite side of the road, with a man in civilian dress crouched near it in the hedge, I was about to fire on him when he saw me, and stood up with his hands raised. He said his name was Quigley, and that he had been trying to get in touch with us to warn us of the coming of the police convoy. Actually I did not believe him, and somehow – perhaps because he was a tall man – I thought he was connected with the police, but as there was a doubt in the matter I told him to leave his machine where it was, and to clear off across the fields. (I afterwards learned that Mr Quigley was the country surveyor of Meath, a good nationalist and supporter of the Volunteer movement).

THE FIGHT AT ASHBOURNE:
THE FINAL SCENES

by Major J.V. Lawless, Cavalry Corps

The Engagement

Having posted the men in what vantage points there were, I reconnoitred the opposite side of the road from a point opposite our position, I found, however, that the bank was so high and steep on that side that it did not offer a good fire position, but I had satisfied myself that there was no enemy on that side.

All this time sporadic firing was going on between our men around the crossroads and the police; one of our party had received a bad scalp wound, and another man (the one with the grenade) had taken him back to the dressing station. This left only four men with myself, and as nearly an hour had elapsed since our arrival in position, with still no sign of the promised attack, I was again beginning to get rather anxious. One of the men (a very young lad with only a shot-gun), was put to watch the main road in our rear, that is, north-westwards; the others began re-arranging positions with a view to bringing fire to bear on the police positions. While doing this, another man had his clothing perforated by a bullet, which showed that our position was observed by the enemy, and so we decided to open upon our own account. Lying on the roadside, sheltered by a low bank, I was able to bring an enfilading fire to bear on the enemy, while the others raked the deep ditch behind the hedge, where most of the police were.

The act of opening fire was a great relief from the continual waiting, and we became emboldened to creep closer to the police and so get better effect from our fire. A bullet striking the road in front of my face, however, blinded me with sand and I had to get back to get my eye cleaned out, one other man keeping up occasional shots. Suddenly the alarm was given that the enemy were advancing along the roadside upon our rear, and were then almost upon us. Through the bushes appeared the flesh colour of faces of men creeping rapidly and purposefully towards us. Leaning over backwards I fired my rifle at the faces, but slipped down before I could fire again. A volley from the enemy raked our position, without doing any damage. We replied, firing as rapidly as possible. Our rifle ammunition was all but expended; only one man still had a good supply, but as his rifle was a 9 m/m Mauser, his supply was of no help to the rest of us. I had a service Webley revolver, with about twenty or thirty rounds, so the others cleared out down the ditch in the direction from which we had come, while the man with the Mauser and myself covered their retreat.

An Unfortunate Error

Bullets were burrowing into the banks around us pretty thickly though we had seen nothing of the enemy except the faces through the bushes. One of the lads moving back down the ditch then shouted that someone was moving towards us on the field side of the road ditch, so running back to him I peered cautiously over the brink of the ditch, just in time to see a pair of boots disappear behind a furze bush about sixty or seventy yards up along the road ditch. I emptied my revolver a couple of times towards this bush, urging the others to hurry. Finding they had halted I went to the leading man, to find that he had come to a gateway crossing the ditch, and was nervous of exposing himself to cross this obstacle, so jumping up and calling on the others to follow, I dived headlong into the ditch on the other side. No one followed, though I again called on them to come on. Suddenly the firing stopped, and there was a lot of confused shouting from which I concluded that the position had been rushed and the other men captured. As my ammunition was now all expended I couldn't do anything about it. So I ran down the ditch, taking the first ditch which turned to the right and so made my way back to the by-road from which we had started (at 'D' on sketch, see page 126).

Here I met the No. 2 section commander who had received a slight wound in the eye, and had come back to the dressing station at the house 'E'. I got five or ten rounds of rifle ammunition from him and in consultation with Dr Hayes and Ashe who came along just then we decided, with the help of another man who was further up the road, to move the bicycles and Hayes' car which lined the road from within a few yards of the crossroads, back as far as the house at 'E', so that we might have some chance of saving them in the retreat which then seemed inevitable.

Ashe went towards the crossroads to order the retreat, and did in fact give the order, which was in process of being carried out, when Mulcahy appeared on the scene. Being told by Dr Hayes what was afoot, he then informed us, to our great surprise and my considerable discomfiture, that the enemy reinforcements we had exchanged shots with, were, in fact, our 4th section, with my father, which had come up from the camp at Borranstown, and was being conducted to our position at 'C' by Mulcahy himself, whose face in the bushes I had fired at.

They had been equally at sea in the matter. Mulcahy knew that we should be thereabouts, but owing to the lapse of time he could not count on what might have happened in the meantime, and our fire was so furious that they felt sure we must be an enemy group and could see them.

However, whether from the excellence of the cover or bad marksmanship, no one had been hit in the exchange, and Mulcahy rushed off after Ashe to have him countermand the retreat order. Apparently there had been considerable difficulty in getting the Volunteers out of their positions at the crossroads, owing to the fire which was being kept up by the police, and, fortunately as it happened, this had slowed up our retreat, so that when Mulcahy got there he was in time to get all the Volunteers back in their original positions, without any intention having been disclosed to the enemy.

Moving on towards the crossroads, I found one of our men at a gateway on the right (about position 'F') having a duel with some police, who apparently were in the ditch on the opposite side of the field. He had just been wounded by a bullet through the forearm, so, sending him back to get it dressed, I took up the firing until, after a little while, there seemed to be no reply to my shots, when I returned to the cottage to try to borrow some more ammunition from the guard in charge of the two prisoners captured in the beginning of the action. With ten more rounds in my magazine I once more headed for the crossroads, picking up another man who had a few rounds of ammunition for his rifle.

'We Surrender'

I again approached the gateway through which I had previously been firing (and I think my attention must have been concentrated on the road ahead), for when the man following me shouted a warning, and jumped for the cover of another gateway beside him, I got the fright of my life to see a policeman crouched on the bank of the ditch on my right, about twenty yards from me. My rifle was slung on my right shoulder, there was no time to seek cover, so I realised when I had got him covered, that I should have been shot twice over, and then I noticed that he was standing up with his hands over his head. Calling on him to keep his hands up and come out on the road, I was further startled to hear a chorus of voices behind him in the ditch shouting 'We surrender'. With no little suspicion and fear of some surprise move, I called to the man behind me to keep them covered, and putting on a bold tone, I ordered the police out on the road.

Eleven burly RIC men, a few of them wounded, and all badly demoralised, lined up on the road. They had thrown away their rifles further up the field, but they had a plentiful supply of ammunition which was a Godsend to us just then.

The prisoners were marched back to the dressing station, where their wounds were attended to by Dr Hayes, and being relived of their belts, ammunition pouches, etc., they were left there under guard of two men, while I hastened towards the crossroads once more to convey the good news that the police were surrendering. I got as far as a point some fifteen or twenty yards from the main road, where I found another of our men firing across the rear of a cottage on the right. He told me he had succeeded in getting one constabulary man who had tried to get through a window into the cottage, and he thought there were others in the bushes above the cottage. With my fresh supply of ammunition I joined him in raking every possible bit of cover there, and then crept on, on hands and knees, towards the main road.

It was difficult to attract the attention of our fellows who were firing from both sides up the main road, east of the crossroads. I had decided to creep under their fire, when I saw the Volunteers nearest me leap across the hedge on to the main road, and run towards the police, with bayonets fixed. Rapidly fixing my own, I doubled around the corner, to meet an amazing sight.

In and out among the cars drawn up on the side of the road,

and along the edge of the bank, and wedged into channel cuttings, were numerous dead and wounded police and drivers; while from out the ditch on the north-eastern side of the road, the remainder of the police were climbing up to the road with their hands over their heads. My father with our 4th section was coming down the road towards us, driving the police from along the ditch in front of them.

The Final Phase

The explanation of the final phase was as follows: when during the incident of our firing upon each other around the position 'C', I had exposed myself to cross the gateway in the ditch, the Volunteers who were firing on us realised their mistake, and hastened to make themselves known to the other men who had been with me. I, however, having mistaken the significance of all the shouting, had run pretty fast, and Mulcahy, realising that it was likely that I would convey a wrong report to the others, followed me, leaving the new section to occupy my old position.

When we had managed to make contact with Ashe, and had retreat order countermanded, he made his way by the fields on the south-western side of the main road, back to the section at 'C'. This section, leaving a few men at 'C', crossed the main road and moved down along the road ditch inside the field, where they were protected from the road by the high bank. Coming to a point about midway in the line of cars on the road, they could hear the officer commanding the police (County Inspector Smith) shouting at the police to get up and fight. He was standing on top of the bank on the opposite side of the road brandishing his revolver and reviling his men for their passivity. Climbing up the bank my father shot him down, but not before he had fired and shot dead one of our men who was behind my father. Smith was undoubtedly a brave man, and the only one of the police who showed a fighting spirit. His death was the signal for a general collapse of the police resistance.

All that remained was to collect the arms, ammunition, and other items of equipment that were of use, and attend to the wounded, some of whom were in pretty bad shape. Ashe then paraded the remaining police under the one officer who was left, and telling them they night return to their homes, he warned them of the consequences should they be found in arms against us. Whereupon we returned to our camp of the night before, and to well-earned food and rest, taking with us the captured arms and other material.

The following general data in connection with the engagement may be of interest:

- The weather on that day was dry with bright sunshine, warm around mid-day, and there was little wind.
- The siege of the barracks commenced about 11.30 a.m.
- Police reinforcements arrived about 12.15 p.m.
- 4th Volunteer section arrived on scene of action about 3 p.m.
- Final surrender of the police about 5 p.m.
- Duration of whole action, therefore, about five and a half hours' continuous fighting.

Number of Volunteers engaged

Originally three sections of approximately twelve men each, total thirty-six; later reinforced by 4th section, twelve. Total number engaged: about forty-eight.

Police engaged

Besieged in barracks, fifteen; (this number was due to the fact, prior to our arrival, the normal garrison had been reinforced, of which we were unaware); reinforcements which arrived in cars approximately seventy to ninety; (the Times Book gives the number as fifty, but there were at least twenty-four large motor cars fully laden, which represents anything from seventy to ninety).

Casualties

Volunteers: two killed, five wounded.

Police: Eight to eleven killed; fifteen to twenty wounded.

In addition to the above, a number of police drivers were killed or wounded.

RESOURCEFULNESS

by Captain Florence O'Donoghue, Infantry Corps

'Battles,' Foch said, 'are won in the soul.' Not in numbers, not in weight of armaments nor in wealth is the decisive element that ensures victory, but in the spirit of men who go into battle with a mentality that will not contemplate or accept defeat.

That mentality, does not blind itself to the strength of the enemy, to his fighting qualities, to his possible superiority in armament, to his wealth or cunning, to his ruthlessness or deceit. It seeks rather to know these things, and many more, about the enemy; to face them honestly; and knowing them to study how best they may be defeated and overcome.

It is no use to theorise about what could be done if one had this or that weapon, unless studying the subject leads to the improvisation of a weapon that can be produced and will give the required effect. It is worse than useless; it is a waste of time and a misdirection of energy which would be better applied to studying the amazing things that can be done with available resources if the best use is made of them. There is always a way of doing seemingly impossible things if we try hard enough to find it. But first there must be a firm conviction that a way can be found.

Leadership inspired by that mentality will raise an army, a battalion or a section to a plane on which it will do heroic things. Every campaign produces examples of what determined and intrepid men can do when their fighting quality is imbued with this spirit.

THE MAN WHO COUNTS

by Theodore Roosevelt

It is not the critic who counts; not the man who points out how the strong man stumbles, or where the doer of deeds could have done them better. The credit belongs to the man who is actually in the arena; whose face is marred by dust and sweat and blood; who strives valiantly; who errs and comes short again and again; because there is no effort without error and shortcoming; who does actually strive to do the deeds; who knows the great enthusiasm, the great devotions; spends himself in a worthy cause; who at the best knows in the end the triumph of high achievement, and who at the worst, if he fails, at least fails while daring greatly, so that his place shall never be with those odd and timid souls who know neither victory nor defeat.

BURNING OF THE DUBLIN CUSTOM HOUSE:

A GRAPHIC ACCOUNT OF A HISTORIC EXPLOIT

by Commandant M. O'Kelly, Infantry Corps

On 25 May 1921, the Irish Republican Army accomplished the total destruction of the Dublin Custom House, thereby paralysing British civil administration in this country.

The scheme had its origin at a meeting of the headquarters staff of the Republican forces held at The O'Rahilly's house, 40 Herbert Park, Dublin. The purpose of the meeting was to discuss the military situation, and the following were present: Cathal Brugha, Michael Collins, Austin Stack, Richard Mulcahy. Pierce Beasley, Gearóid O'Sullivan, J.J. O'Connell, Seán McMahon, Seán Russell, Liam Mellows, Eamon de Valera.

They were all agreed that the time had come to deliver a smashing blow at England – to undertake some bigger military operation than anything yet attempted.

Two Projects

Two projects were laid before the conference: the taking of Beggars'

Bush Barracks, a strong military position in the hands of the enemy or the destruction of the Custom House; both these suggestions came from President de Valera.

The following government departments were housed in the Custom House: Inland Revenue, Local Government, Estate Duty Control Registers, Stamp Office, Income Tax and Joint Stock Company Registers.

Its destruction would reduce the most important branch of British civil government in Ireland to virtual impotence and would, in addition, inflict on her a financial loss of about two million pounds.

The officer commanding the Dublin Brigade was ordered to investigate the relative merits of the two schemes and a member of the intelligence department was ordered to take up his residence in a house opposite Beggars' Bush Barracks and make his report. This report, received in due course, expressed the view that to take this strongly fortified position by surprise was almost impossible, and after some deliberation the Custom House operation was decided upon.

A Clever Ruse

The officer commanding Dublin Brigade was successful in carrying out a personal reconnaissance of the building. Carrying some envelopes in his hand, he entered the building one day and, under the pretext of looking for someone in one of the numerous departments, made his way through the huge building without arousing any suspicion, thus making the fixing of details possible.

A ground plan of the building was copied from one in the National Library.

Commandant T. Ennis, officer commanding 2nd Battalion, was appointed to take charge. He was informed he could have the pick of the brigade. The number required to carry out the job was estimated at one hundred and twenty. This number did not include a covering party for outside nor a guard for the city Fire Brigade stations, which were provided for by the officer commanding the brigade. The Units actually engaged inside the building were the 2nd Battalion and ASU; while outside was a section of the 1st Battalion.

The opinion was expressed by the president that if these one hundred and twenty men were lost and the job accomplished, the sacrifice would be well justified.

Equipment

The material required for the operation was: two hundred and eighty gallons of paraffin oil, one hundred and forty tins of petrol and two bales of cotton-waste. All these had to be procured at the earliest possible moment, and accordingly the O/C, 'B' Coy, 2nd Battalion, was detailed to commandeer the paraffin and petrol. The O/C, 'D' Coy, 2nd Battalion, was to get the tins and cotton waste a week prior to the operation, which had been fixed for 25 May 1921. Both these officers were successful in getting the material. The paraffin and petrol was got by holding up horse-drawn tanks in the streets and making prisoners of the drivers, the tins, by carrying out a raid on the Shell Company's yard, and the waste from the Broadstone Railway Station. The process of filling the petrol tins was started immediately at one of the company dumps. The other equipment necessary was as follows: hatchets, bolt-cutters and transport, these being left over until the morning of 25 May.

Assembly

Oriel Hall was the assembly point. Orders were issued to report there at 12 noon on 25 May, and accordingly the boys drifted along

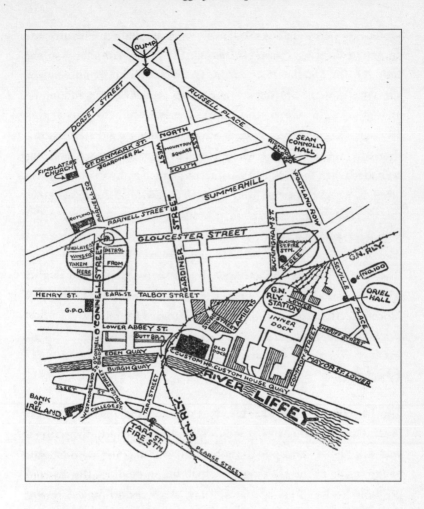

in the usual groups of two's and three's. It was, however, observed by the first few to arrive that the goods' yard of the GN Railway was occupied by the enemy, some of whom were actually leaning over the wall overlooking Oriel Hall. Word to this effect was despatched to the battalion commander at 100 Seville Place, who immediately gave orders to have the assembly point changed to Seán Connolly Hall.

It was about 12.15 p.m. when the last man arrived at the new

R⁰ᵐˢ

venue. 'The Manager', by which name Commandant T. Ennis was known to all, was present. He had already given instructions to the O/C, 'D' Coy, 2nd Battalion, earlier on that morning to commandeer a heavy motor lorry, proceed to the dump, load the stores and report to him at 12.15 p.m. at the venue. The lorry duly arrived at this moment. This car was commandeered from outside Findlater's shop in O'Connell Street, where it had been in the process of being unloaded when the O/C, 'D' Coy, accompanied by his driver and one other, came on the scene. They were all agreed that the vehicle met the necessary requirements, so the officer in charge informed the men who were unloading, as politely as he could, that he required the car for a few hours. The men handed over the car without any fuss, whereupon the vehicle was driven to the dump and loaded with the stores. This done, it was driven to Connolly Hall, where all officers, section leaders and men were paraded for orders.

Orders

The battalion commander briefly explained the operation to all present and told them what was required of them, also the result it was expected to have upon the enemy. He was in possession of a plan of the inside of the building by which he pointed out the allotted positions to be taken up upon entry, at the same time detailing the officers for each floor. There were four company commanders present, one of these (O/C, 'D' Coy), being appointed second in command. The route was outlined and the following orders issued: the guard to enter at 12.58 p.m., man all entrances, dismantle telephonic communication, allow in all persons who desired but allow no one to leave, and make prisoners of the two policemen at the main entrance. The lorry to be at this entrance at 12.59 p.m.

Every man was to be possession of a hatchet on arrival. They would raid likely shops on the way for these.

The main body was to enter at 1 p.m.; on arrival at the main entrance each man to take two 2-gallon tins of petrol off the lorry. They would then proceed to allotted corridors, instruct the members of the staff to collect all personal belongings and proceed to the main hall, taking particular care that no person pocketed any official documents; close all windows, smash all presses, collect all papers in a heap on the floor and thoroughly soak the floor and all inflammable material with petrol. As each floor was ready for firing, the officer in charge of the floor was to report the fact to inform the battalion commander, who would give the orders to set fire, starting at the top floor. In order to guard against possible confusion, it was strictly forbidden for any man to have a whistle in his possession.

In the event of any hitch occurring that would prevent the job being finished, the battalion commander would give a whistle-blast, which would be the signal for every man to get away.

This completed the orders, and all proceeded in the direction of the Custom House by the routes indicated.

Protection

Every man was armed with a revolver and six rounds of ammunition.

The officer commanding Dublin Brigade had arranged for a covering party to be posted on the railway bridge over looking the Custom House. He also had men posted in all Fire Brigade stations, to prevent their being of assistance to the enemy.

Operation

At 1 p.m. (the appointed time) the party converged on the Custom

House from the direction of Store Street, Gardiner Street and Amiens Street. There were a large number of people about at the time, it being the mid-day rush hour, therefore the various groups of men passed unnoticed. The success of the operation depended on the elements of surprise and speed, but unfortunately a lot of time was lost in the herding of the staff to the main hall. All of them were completely surprised at the audacity of the attack. The suddenness with which the building was entered threw them into a state of panic, though at first some were inclined to take the whole thing as a joke. On seeing the number of guns in evidence, however, they realised that real business was intended. Others who were stout supporters of the enemy administration were very reluctant to do as ordered, and here a little gentle persuasion was necessary.

The lady members of the staff in particular became panicky and hysterical and a considerable amount of time was lost on this account. The caretaker rushed to the telephone, although previously warned against doing so, and had to be shot. The enemy were, however, warned from some unknown source, with the result that they arrived in strength at 1.17 p.m., seventeen minutes after the building had been entered and before preparations for firing had been completed.

The first lorry to arrive was engaged by the covering party from the railway bridge with grenade and revolver fire. (According to official reports four Tans were wounded.)

The unexpected had happened, and the men inside, on hearing the shooting, took upon position at the doors and windows and opened up on the enemy, who were also taking up positions.

At this time excitement was running high among the staff. Above the din could be heard the blast of a whistle; this came from one of the attackers, who apparently had become excited, too.

Mistaken Signal

The men on the top landing, on hearing the whistle and thinking it was the whistle to get away, rushed to the ground floor towards the main entrance. Just at this time the battalion commander appeared in the main hall and realised that his original plan had miscarried through one of the men giving a blast on a whistle contrary to orders. He, with characteristic decision, ordered Lieutenant J. Slattery, who was posted at the main entrance, to close the door. He then ordered all men from the main hall upstairs, at the same time giving the order to 'set fire'. The promptness with which the battalion commander acted saved the situation and succeeded in re-establishing control when all looked like being lost. The men, for their part, giving ready obedience to their leader, rushed up the stairs after him and set about the task of destroying the top portion of the building with thoroughness, leaving nothing to chance. By the time they had completed their task the second floor had also been set alight and it was only with the greatest difficulty, fighting through the blinding smoke, that they succeeded in making their way back to the ground floor.

The building was now completely surrounded by the enemy. The Black and Tans had been reinforced by military, who were keeping up a continuous fire on the building with machine guns from armoured cars which they had brought into position underneath the railway bridge.

A number of casualties occurred among the staff from stray bullets coming through the windows and doors (newspaper reports gave one killed and six wounded). The men inside were replying to the fire whenever an inviting target showed up. Some of the ASU (known as the 'Squad') were armed with Peter the Painters, and used them to good advantage.

Critical Position

The position was now becoming impossible inside, with the fire spreading rapidly, so the battalion commander gave the order for everyone to get out. The staff rushed out, shouting: 'friends, friends'. It was a case of every man for himself now, so most of the men, having fired their six rounds, dumped the guns and filed out behind the staff. Once outside, the higher officials of the staff picked out their own, who were set free; the remainder, being all IRA, were placed under a heavy guard to await the arrival of the lorries.

Just at this time there were a few rushes from the building in twos and threes with men trying to fight their way through the cordon.

For most it was a futile effort. A couple were fortunate in getting away, but others were badly wounded, including the battalion commander. His was a miraculous escape, as he was one of the very last to leave the building and had to decide between being burned to death, captured, or chance getting away by a rush. The odds were one in a hundred against getting away. If he were captured it would in all probability mean shooting, he being a very much wanted man. This fact, I think, decided him upon attempting to get away. He selected the only point where the enemy appeared to be weak, and with a gun in each hand made a rush from a side-gate towards the lane opposite; he had only gone about twenty yards when he fell wounded with a bullet in the hip. He picked himself up and made a second dash, firing as he went, was struck again, this time in the leg, but he kept on going as best he could until he arrived at the top of the lane, where he saw a horse drawn cart, into which he scrambled. Luckily, the driver of the cart, who was friendly towards the IRA, recognised him and willingly took him to safety.

Success

The entire operation was successfully carried out in the face of an enemy in superior numbers and fire power and was a hazardous undertaking in itself, calling for a high degree of determination and skill on the part of the commander and of unwavering courage on the part of the remainder.

Casualties

Killed: Captain Paddy O'Reilly, Lieut Stephen O'Reilly, Dan Head, Eddie Dorrins, Seán Doyle; wounded: Comdt T. Ennis. Lieut J. Slattery, J. Ward; taken prisoner: all ranks.

Total enemy casualties are unknown, as the true figures were never published by the British authorities.

Surprise

This operation brings out the element of surprise very forcibly, the importance of striking the enemy at a vital part when he least expects it.

The main nerve-centre of British administration in Ireland was located in the Custom House, and that nerve-centre was completely destroyed in broad day-light, in the midst of a city occupied by a large garrison and ceaselessly patrolled by mobile armed parties.

Protection

A force can be regarded as secure from surprise only when protection is furnished in every direction from which attack is possible. Here the enemy was allowed to get within striking distance of the main body from all directions. The protection afforded was altogether inadequate. Time was the all-important factor in this particular operation, therefore, ambush parties should have been posted at all likely routes for the purpose of gaining that time and holding up the enemy's advance.

Quick Decision

An outstanding lesson to be learned from this operation is the value of quick decision in the leader, as instanced in this case, where we see Commandant T. Ennis, suddenly confronted with a situation which threatened to imperil the success of the action, display the qualities that make a leader, in the rapidity with which he make his decision and turned what might have been failure into success.

THE DROMKEEN AMBUSH:
AN ACTION OF THE BLACK AND TAN PERIOD

by Major J.M. McCarthy, GHQ

Flaunting defiance from the highest point of a large, detached building in the village of Pallas,* County Limerick, a conspicuous flag in the sombre colours of black and tan strikingly, if unconventionally, identified the local police barracks throughout the winter of 1920–1921. Here, also, was housed the headquarters of a police district in charge of an officer ranking as a district inspector, RIC, but whose special category, and that of the greater part of the large garrison, was plainly indicated by the unofficial emblem so prominently displayed. The hoisting of this banner reflected fairly well the tension prevailing in the area at that period, and was expressive of the challenging sentiments of the garrison towards the countryside at large, but particularly towards the East and Mid-Limerick Brigades, IRA. These two units were equally involved through the fact that, though Pallas itself was in the East Limerick domain, the

---

* *Author's Note*: This is the form of the name by which the village is normally known except when necessary to distinguish it from Old Pallas, one and a half miles to the south-west. According to local usage, it then becomes New Pallas. The Ordnance Survey map versions are respectively Pallas Green (New) and Pallas Green, but in some map editions Old Pallas is given as an alternative to the latter name. This is a fair example of the confusion that can sometimes arise in relating map references to local usage, and of the pitfalls to be watched for in that connection.

inter-brigade boundary ran close by, while the police district and, needless to say, the police activities extended into both areas.

For long the operations, and more especially the methods, of the garrison, besides making its personnel exceptionally feared by the general public, had proved a very sharp thorn for the two brigades and faced them with a challenge that had to be met. The police were definitely in the ascendant when, early in 1921, they scored what, in the circumstances of the times, was a big success, and for the local IRA a correspondingly serious reverse; by locating and capturing the arms dump of the Mid-Limerick Brigade. Incidentally, the police raiding party took care to celebrate their feat by visiting the house of the 'on-the-run' C/O of the brigade's active service column, and staging a *feu-de-joie* with the captured weapons in the presence of the occupants paraded to witness, so they were assured, this proof of defeat and final end of the column's activities.

These events brought matters to a head. Consultations, already in progress between the two brigade staffs with a view to common action, were hastened to a conclusion. Plans were considered for an attack on the barracks but, in view of the pitiably poor armament of the IRA, disclosed serious difficulties to be surmounted. The nature of the building, its position and defences made for difficulty of approach, and ensured a protracted fight if the defenders were to be overcome. Despite the fairly extensive experience of the East Limerick column in conducting prolonged and successful barrack attacks, such as that at Kilmallock in the previous May, when the attack was sustained for over six hours, the time factor in this case was a definite obstacle to success. The proximity of Pallas to large military and police centres (Limerick city, ten miles, Tipperary, twelve miles) made it probable that the garrison would be relieved long before the barracks could be destroyed or captured, notwithstanding all that might be done to impede the arrival of reinforcements. With a mere sniping, or demonstration, attack being of no value, since the situation required that the IRA should register a clear-cut success,

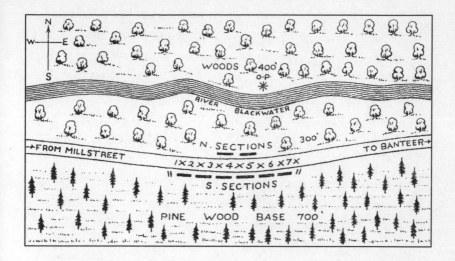

an awkward problem seemed to defy solution when the IO of the Mid-Limerick column came to the rescue. He was able to report that a considerable portion of the Pallas police garrison regularly travelled with a lorry-convoy to Fedamore, eleven miles distant, making the return journey on the same day. Further, he was able to indicate the route normally followed, and even to fix the usual date of the movement as the first Thursday of each month.

Decision to attack Convoy

With this information the decision to attack and destroy this convoy was taken, the first Thursday of February being fixed for the effort as a joint operation by East and Mid-Limerick columns. An examination of the route led to the further conclusion that a carefully laid ambush along a particular stretch of road (see sketch) at Dromkeen, some three miles from Pallas, offered the best method of attack. Here a straight section of the route extended for three hundred yards, slightly downhill, from a bend at its western (Fedamore) end to a road junction at its eastern (Pallas) limit. Dromkeen House at the

155

bend afforded observation both over the whole ambush position, and westward for a considerable distance towards Fedamore. The road junction presented almost full right-angled turns to vehicles travelling in any direction, and was an obvious site for barricades which would be out of sight until the turn was about to be taken. From this point, too, observation over the entire position, and extending as far as the western bend and Dromkeen House, was feasible from a ruined house at the road fork.

These facilities, and the lay-out of the road section, were definite advantages in the light of a number of factors. The basic decision being to effect complete destruction of the convoy, a fairly lengthy stretch of the route had to be held in order to ensure that all the vehicles were within the position before the action opened. The position had also to be capable of being sealed-off at both ends once the convoy had entered it. The length, at first sight over-long, was therefore not excessive in the circumstances especially when there was no certainty as to the number of lorries likely to be encountered, nor as to the distance between the lorries.

To reduce this uncertain element to the minimum, and for other reasons, it was decided to intercept the convoy on its return, rather than on its outward, journey. In this way its strength would be known on its departure from Pallas and, though it had varied somewhat on occasions, might be counted on to be approximately the same when it set out on its return trip from Fedamore. With this knowledge any necessary last-minute adjustment in dispositions could be made. Further, the later in the day the action opened the better from the standpoint of the column's withdrawal, which it was desired to effect under cover of darkness as far as possible in view of the elaborate military and police reactions anticipated. The other grounds for interception on the return journey were that it made actual occupation of the position unnecessary until confirmation of the movement of the convoy was received, and by that very fact, lessened the possibility of a long and perhaps fruitless wait in the position itself. Also, by ensuring that occupation would not be affected at all if the convoy did not move out, possible disclosure of intentions was avoided, and the same site could be used another day. This alternative was important in view of the suitability of the location, and the distinct chance that the Intelligence Officer's estimate as to the date of the movement might not be borne out by events.

Keeping this valuable alternative in mind, as well as the special caution needed in this particular area, the arrival of the two columns, and their junction with one another, was so timed that neither would be in the immediate vicinity of Pallas longer than was absolutely necessary. The most distant of the two, the East Limerick unit, was mainly concerned in this 'approach march'. By the day preceding that fixed for the attack it had reached a billeting area, nine miles away, near Emly, on the Limerick-Tipperary border. At nightfall it moved forward some four miles to the neighbourhood of Kilteely. Here it remained for a few hours before continuing, while still dark, to a previously agreed on 'assembly area' and rendezvous with the Mid Limerick column.

The Columns make Contact

At this point, situated in a secluded locality away from dwellings, and a little over a mile short of the selected Dromkeen position, contact was made between the two columns just before dawn. The combined force, some forty riflemen strong, then lay up to await developments, a dilapidated shed affording the shelter needed both because of secrecy and because of the fact that the weather during the moves on the preceding nights had been very bad and had so continued. Communication was soon established with the local scouts who, from early morning, were keeping movements in Pallas, and on the adjoining roads, under observation. It was not however, until close to noon that calculations were in great part fulfilled by the news that two lorries, carrying about twenty policemen, with the district inspector in charge, had started out along the road towards Fedamore.

Dispositions

A move was at once made to the site for the intended interception through which, as further information soon indicated, the lorries had passed, travelling fast and close together. The weather had now cleared, and luckily, as matters developed, little time was required for taking up positions, these having been assigned beforehand. Excepting the farm house at the turn of the road to Old Pallas, all the houses and the barn shown in the sketch provided fire positions, and were occupied in varying strength according to accommodation and field of fire available. The farmhouse, left unoccupied, was used to detain passers-by, some half-dozen being thus 'interned'. Dromkeen House, on road bend at the western end, held a party detailed to observe the route towards Fedamore, signal movements from that direction, and prevent a withdrawal by the lorries or their occupants by that route. What amounted to the CP [command post] was set up in the ruined house facing the road-junction. Small detachments also took position at intervals on both sides of the straight stretch of road along its low boundary walls, in the yard of the farm-house used as 'a place of detention', and at the fences covering the road-fork and two barricades erected there. These barricades were made with farm-carts in preference to other forms of obstruction so that no outward signs need have remained should there have been a postponement. For the same reason no artificial fire positions were constructed except at the northern boundary wall of the road where loose stones, readily replaceable, permitted a limited number of loop-holes. Elsewhere fire was to be brought to

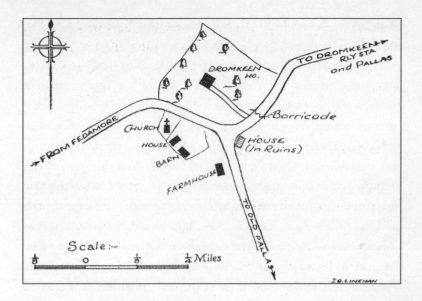

bear from the top of the walls and the fences, the hay in the barn, and the windows of the houses.

These steps completed the dispositions except for two other measures intended to secure the authors of the projected surprise against being themselves surprised. One was the occupation by a party of armed local Volunteers of a position near Dromkeen across the intended line of retreat to keep open that route and cover the withdrawal of the column. This step was considered essential in view of the heavy military traffic in the vicinity. The other security measure was the use of a screen of scouts provided over a wide area by the local Volunteer companies to warn of hostile approach from an unexpected direction. The frequency of enemy patrols in the locality generally, and on the main Limerick-Tipperary road, only three-quarter mile distant, made such an outcome not improbable. Whether or not it was appreciated at the time, the fact is however, that these scouts had no effective means of delaying, or rapidly communicating the progress of any hostile formation should the latter, as was likely, have been motorised. Consequently, had an

159

occasion for action by the scouts arisen, this protective measure would in all probability have broken down badly.

It was now a little after 12.30 p.m. with all in readiness. After an uncomfortable night and morning, and a seventeen-mile cross-country march to their next billeting area in prospect, the Volunteers hoped for an early end to their vigil. In this they were not disappointed, for nearing one o'clock the approach of lorries was signalled for Dromkeen House. Hardly had the signal been amplified to indicate the number of vehicles as two, when the first lorry appeared around the road bend, quickly followed by the second at about fifty yards distance. Orders had provided for the opening of fire when the first of whatever number of lorries might compose the convoy took the turn at the road-junction. In the event, fire was opened a few seconds before this occurred, due probably to the riflemen in the western half of the position having difficulty in judging the exact moment of the leading lorry's arrival at the road fork. As matters were, this was of no consequence, though it might have been otherwise had there been a larger convoy, or a wider interval between the lorries. This point, however, serves to emphasise the necessity of a checking up on details lest the larger plan be wrecked through a small oversight.

The Convoy Engaged

After the opening volley, the first lorry continued along the short distance separating it from the road-junction. Confronted with the barricade as he was taking the left-hand turn on the usual route – that leading to Dromkeen Station – the driver swerved violently to the right in an effort to take the other turn. Faced here with the second barricade the lorry struck both it and the fence adjoining the ruined house. Thrown, or jumping clear, the driver, who happened to be the district inspector, and another policeman, both unwounded, reached the adjoining field. Aided by the fact that they alone among the police party were wearing civilian clothes, they succeeded in making good their escape, and eventually proved to be the sole survivors of a total police party of thirteen. A stronger police escort had been expected, but a reduction in the original number had probably been made at Fedamore. Of the fire occupants of the first lorry three remained, one of whom was mortally, and two slightly, wounded at the outset. The latter two took cover at the roadside, but shortly after were against hit, this time fatally.

The second lorry contained eight policemen. It had arrived a little beyond mid-way in the ambush position when the first shots were fired. Halting at once its occupants began to dismount. Some were hit while doing so, others as they took up positions at the roadside. Five were killed outright, and one sustained severe wounds that proved fatal some days later. Two managed to get into positions beneath the lorry. From here, firing from behind the wheels, and refusing to surrender, they maintained a steady exchange of shots. Difficult to hit in this situation, they were eventually struck and killed by fire brought to bear from new positions on the road level taken up by a few of the attackers. In passing, it is both of interest, and fitting to record here that the two policemen responsible for this determined fight against hopeless odds were two of the only three members of the 'regular' RIC in the police party. It was in the course of the attack on this second lorry that the Volunteers sustained their single casualty, a Volunteer officer on the wall near the church having his hand shattered by a bullet.

This casualty somewhat complicated the pre-arranged cross-country withdrawal and the 'evasive action' to counter the widespread military and police 'round-up' that now ensured. For a great part of the march various forms of transport had to be called on to permit the wounded officer keeping up with the column. By using field-paths and avenues, however, the move was effected, with the result that nightfall saw the Volunteers safely through the cordons and installed in billets some seventeen miles from Dromkeen.

Lessons

To draw lessons from this operation is not to attach undue importance to what, by the ordinary scale of war, was a very minor affair indeed. But all combat actions, big or little, successes or failures, point a moral worth seeking. In this case the lessons might be summarised as follows:

Information

The action is an instance of good intelligence work, of the essential contribution made to success by this factor, and or how careful observation and the collection of bits and scraps of information – a task often monotonous and seemingly futile – becomes a formidable weapon yielding valuable results. LDF intelligence personnel, in particular, take note!

Secrecy

The nature of the operation of course automatically required secrecy. But the special pains taken bring out the point that, subject to the prompt execution of the task, no trouble is too great to take in order to prevent disclosure of one's plans or intentions.

Surprise

Even if this, too, was an inherent element in the type of action it would not have been so complete in the absence of foresight and measures specifically aimed at its achievement. With surprise a basic principle of war applicable to all forms of action, and one of the surest roads to success, its aid must be sought in some shape or other in every situation.

Security

Both sides committed faults under this head. The police escort obviously made two grave errors in continually using the same route, and keeping the lorries so close together. Thereby they largely contributed to the completeness of the surprise, and to the hopelessness of their position from the start. This 'bunching', whether of transport or personnel, seems to be a general human failing common to all times, places and conditions. Nowadays, it is still prevalent in face of the much greater penalties modern warfare would exact. On the part of the Volunteers, security was provided for in theory, but in practice the steps taken against their being themselves the victim of the unexpected were defective. The point here is not that elaborate precautions were either essential or feasible in the situation, but that unreliable protective measures can be more dangerous than none at all through giving rise to a false sense of security.

Co-operation

Dromkeen was in effect a 'limiting-point' on an inter-unit boundary. For LDF areas and districts especially, the operation teaches avoidance of watertight compartment methods, and depicts the value of – in fact the necessity for – close contact and teamwork with adjoining units.

Endurance and Determination

The stand made by the remnant of the escort in the second lorry typifies the will to fight on in a desperate situation, or, in other words, 'resistance to the last man and to the last round'. If no exceptional display of the qualities of endurance and determination was called for on the IRA side, the acceptance by the Volunteers of a fair amount of discomfort and fatigue, the better to carry out their self-imposed mission, goes to show that there is nothing unreasonable in expecting hundred-fold greater exertions from their present-day LDF successes who, the numerous and official instruments of an established state, in contrast with the few scattered guerrilla bands who established it, are incomparably better organised, trained, armed and equipped than the IRA of 1920–1921.

> The results on which we count in warfare are never as precise as is imagined by someone who has not carefully observed a war and become used to it.
>
> Very often we miscalculate the march of a column by several hours, without being able to tell the cause of the delay. Often we encounter obstacles which were impossible to foresee. Often we intend to reach a certain place with our army and fall short of it by several hours. Often a small outpost which we have set up achieves much less than we expected, while an enemy outpost achieves much more. Often the resources of a region do not amount to as much as we expected, etc.
>
> We can triumph over such obstacles only with very great exertion, and to accomplish this the leader must show a severity bordering on cruelty. Only when he knows that everything possible is always being done, can he be sure that these small difficulties will not have a great influence on his operations. Only then can he be sure that he will not fall too far short of the aim which he could have reached.
>
> Carl von Clausewitz

THE ARMY BADGE

(Reprinted from *An t-Óglach*)

When, some twenty-five years ago now, our Gaelic scholars were casting about for a fitting and worthy name for the infant Volunteer organisation, the name of 'Fianna Fáil' was suggested by the late Canon Peadar O'Leary. No greater authority could be quoted in support of any matter pertaining to the Irish Language than that of the 'Leomhan na Gaoluinne,' and, surely, it would be difficult to furnish a more appropriate title to designate the fighting forces of the Gael than the two words represented by the letters, FF.

Fianna

The word 'Fianna' to the Irish mind is symbolic of the valour, manly prowess and chivalry of our race, while 'Fáil' is bound up with the very earliest political and religious systems of the ancient Gael.

The name Fianna was first applied to the great military organisation founded in the third century by the celebrated Fionn Mac Cumhaill himself, and has been used more than seventeen hundred years as a synonym for the Gael militant. At various periods also it has been used to designate the advocates and defenders of Ireland's rights and liberties.

The Fianna were revered and honoured almost as gods by the hero-worshipping Gael, and were looked upon by him as the embodiment of all that was brave, noble and generous. The poets and bards of the Gael have sung their praises in countless songs; the great bulk of our national literature is founded on the exploits of the heroes and chiefs of the Fianna, and their names are forever enshrined in the topography of the country. Aspirants for its ranks were obliged to undergo searching tests as to their mental as well as their physical qualifications. Fionn, Ossian [*sic*], Oscar [*sic*], Diarmaid and many other celebrated leaders of the organisation were poets as well as warriors.

The old semi-military organisation was John O'Mahony's ideal for an Irish army, and Pádraig Pearse dreamed of an Irish army combining, like the Fianna of old, Gaelic culture with all the Gaelic reverence for magnanimous courage, justice and honour.

Fál

The innumerable legends and traditions associated

with the magic word 'Fál' transport us back to the remote, prehistoric period of the De Danaan occupation of the country. The celebrated Lia Fáil was brought hither by them when they first decided on the conquest of Erin. This 'Stone of Destiny' was one of their most jealously guarded treasures. It was worshipped and revered, not only by the De Danaans, but by their Milesian successors to the sovereignty of Ireland, as a gift of the gods. For centuries the coronation ceremonies of the Gaelic monarchs were performed on this Lia Fáil, and the Gaels had implicit faith in all the extraordinary powers attributed to their magic Stone of Destiny. It was credited with the power of emitting sounds when the rightful heir to the throne was crowned, and thus assured that none but the legitimate successor could attain to the kingship.

When the sons of Earc, having established an Irish colony in Scotland, found themselves sufficiently strong to assert their rights to the sovereignty of that country, Feargus, the first of the kings thus selected, applied to his brother, who was then Ard Rí of Ireland, for a loan of the Lia Fáil so that the ceremony of the coronation might be performed with all the religious solemnity and with all the rites and pomp with which such ceremonies had been, for thousands of years, performed by his ancestors.

The Lia Fáil was thus transported to Scotland, and there it remained, in the monastery of the

Scone until the reign of Edward I of England. This monarch, in one of his incursions into the territory of his northern neighbours, had the Lia Fáil seized and carried off to England. It is believed by the many excellent authorities that the large stone in the coronation chair at Westminster was the original Lia Fáil.

From this Lia Fáil Ireland received one of its ancient names, Inis Fáil. This is the origin of the well-known 'Innisfail,' the anglicised form popularised by Moore.

'FOUR RIFLEMEN ENTERED INNISHANNON'
INTENSIFIED GUERRILLA WARFARE IN 1921

The following is the actual report of the activities of the 3rd Cork Brigade, IRA, on 14 May 1921. The original was recently recovered from an old dump. It shows how the principles of guerrilla warfare as discussed from time to time in these page were put into practice in West Cork in 1921.

The report is as follows:

Cork No. 3, Brigade.
20/3/21.

(1) Four riflemen entered Innishannon. On arriving at the village no police were about, but one was seen outside the village and shot dead at one hundred and fifty yards range.

(2) Five riflemen entered Kilbrittain and took up a position outside the village. On hearing of a enemy column being in the neighbourhood, they abandoned hat position and took a position in front of the barrack and fired on two policemen at the barrack door, they killed one and seriously wounded another.

(3) Nine riflemen and five revolver-men entered Courtmac-sherry. The riflemen were holding the military station while

five revolver-men searched the village. The revolver-men engaged three soldiers, killed one and seriously wounded another. The third escaping. Two soldiers were also fired on at long range but escaped.

(4) It was arranged that four men armed with guns and revolvers should go to the Old Road Station at the spot where the men were to mobilise. The enemy column under Major Percival appeared. Only the captain of Ballinspittle had arrived at the mobilisation point at the time having three rifles and ammunition and also two revolvers. Major Percival seeing him opened fire on him emptying two revolvers, but did not succeed in hitting him. He engaged Percival who was two hundred yards away from his men, and knocked him with his second shot. He then got away saving his rifles, ammunition and revolvers.

(5) Five men, four riflemen and a Lewis Gun driving in a motor car (their intention being to enter Bandon) came on a military outpost who were guarding a party of military and police at recreation, at about three hundred yards from the military and police barracks. One soldier was killed and two others wounded including a Black and Tan. They held their position for about ten minutes and then left in the motor car. No casualties were inflicted on our side.

(6) Clonakilty was entered at 3 p.m. by a party of nine riflemen who came from the western side of the town and a party of five revolver-men from the southern side. The party of riflemen fired on three policemen at a distance of three hundred yards, but were unable to inflict any casualties. The party of revolver-men were not able to get into action. The whole party remained in town for half-an-hour and then retired.

(7) Dunmanway was entered by three sections of men, one from the north side, one from the southern side, and one from the western side, the total strength being sixteen riflemen, six shot-gun men and six revolver-men. All three

parties proceeded towards market square and searched public houses and hotels on their way. When the first section reached the market square, they sighted four policemen walking in their direction in twos with about fifty yards between each pair. The party opened fire on them, but two ran into a public house, one of the other two fled and the other appeared to be wounded, both of them however, managed to retreat towards the police barracks which was only about eighty yards from them. The two who entered the public house were followed, the house searched but the police had made their escape through a back door. The whole party remained in town for half-an-hour and then retired.

No casualties were inflicted on our side.

(Signed)

Commandant

NA FIANNA ÉIREANN
SENIOR CORPS OF THE OLD ARMY

by Major General Hugh MacNeill

A Celtic Twilight

Na Fianna Éireann has been described as the 'Senior Corps of the Old Army'. To many readers that will not convey much. We have got to ask ourselves just what was this Fianna Éireann.

It was a Boy Scout organisation, but a Boy Scout organisation with a difference. In the first place it was the first open Irish military organisation in this century. For its strength it probably did more than any other organisation to make the Ireland of today and the army of today possible. That sounds like a tall story but a check back on the facts recorded in this article will, it is believed, prove it. Only facts, not fancies, are recorded.

It is necessary at the beginning that we get a true picture of the Ireland which saw the birth of the Fianna. It is very difficult for young soldiers, who were not born at the time to visualise the Ireland of 1909, the year in which the Fianna was formed. To begin with one lived in what was almost a British province, almost as alien in rule and to some extent in outlook as Lancashire or Yorkshire. There was, of course, no Irish government of any type. A foreign viceroy ruled in the Phoenix Park, foreign officials governed from Dublin

Castle, foreign soldiers occupied our garrisons, foreign controlled police patrolled our towns and villages. Our education, our money, everything of outward significance was foreign. That was just thirty-five short years ago.

It is true that our people had never tamely accepted this foreign domination. They had struggled and protested and fought against it for a week of centuries. But there was not much fight left in them in the early part of this century – or at least there did not seem to be. In the preceding hundred years no less than four attempts at armed revolt had gone down in disaster. The United Irishmen failed in 1798, Robert Emmet in 1803, the Young Irelanders in 1848, the Fenians in 1867. Ireland seemed tired and weary of fighting.

The people had turned instead to what were known as constitutional methods. The Irish Party, under the leadership of Mr John Redmond were by argument and persuasion, mainly in the British House of Commons, trying to win a limited amount of local government known as Home Rule.

The real national movements were mainly of a cultural, industrial, or sporting nature. Arthur Griffith was preaching his policy of Sinn Féin, but he and his handful of followers were looked on as insignificant cranks. The Gaelic League were struggling to revive interest in Irish, but few listened to them. The Irish Theatre (now the world-famous Abbey) were trying to get people to come to Irish plays, but few went. There was an attempt to revive Irish industry, but few bought home goods. The Gaelic Athletic Association was trying to develop hurling and Gaelic football, but it was a mere shadow of the powerful nationwide organisation we known today.

It was not a very thrilling or inspiring country to live in, this Ireland of 1909. It was, in fact a pretty good example of the 'Celtic Twilight', the poets used to sing of in another connection.

Birth of the Fianna

Then a little group of people hit on a new idea. They felt that their generation was worn out, nationally at least, and that all hope lay in the future. They realised that Ireland's greatest trouble in all her struggles lay in her lack of trained leaders. They decided to train the boys of that generation as the leaders of the future. It seemed a mad dream then, but it was dream which was to come true within a few short years.

Who were these far-seeing patriots? Many of their names have since gone down to fame. Pádraig Pearse for example, later leader of the Volunteers in 1916, teacher not alone of the boys of Ireland, but of their nation. Roger Casement who was to die seven years later on an English scaffold. Liam Mellows, who was later to die too, but in the tragedy of Civil War.

But strange to say the real inspiration behind the new movement was not a man at all, it was a woman. This was Constance, Countess de Markievicz, 'Madam' as she was known and loved by thousands of Fianna boys. It was in her keen brain the idea was conceived, it was she translated the dream into reality. For eleven of the twelve years of its heyday, she led the Fianna as *ard fheinnidh* or chief scout. In 1918 the position was held by a young Volunteer officer, one Eamon de Valera.

Madam's name must rank among the great daughters of our race. Born in County Sligo she was a member of the aristocratic Anglo-Irish family of Gore-Booth. Her early upbringing was, of necessity, anti-Irish or at least anti-national. In her youth she was one of the most beautiful girls in society, the belle of the British courts in Dublin and London, the toast of the British garrison. Such was her background.

But as she often told her Feinnidhe she never felt happy in it. The luxury of her father's mansion meant less to her than the honest welcome of a countryman's cabin. Her real childhood friends were the children of the hardy fishermen and farm labourers of the Sligo coast Later on she grew interested in Irish painting and drama, regarded as quite respectable hobbies for a young lady of fashion. It was in these circles she met her husband, Count Casimir Dunin Markievicz, a Pole, and an aristocrat like herself. Living in the fashionable Dublin of those days, she did not forget her poor friends in the west coast. So in addition to her artistic leanings it was natural she should take an interest in the lives of their opposite numbers in the slums of Dublin.

And along this path walked the beautiful young aristocrat to become the pioneer of a National Boys Movement – essentially a movement for poor boys. From this it was a short step to the fires of Easter Week, the chill of a prison cell, and her great share in the proud challenge of a resurgent nation in the years that followed.

The Fenian Traditions

The decision, once made, to form the new body a constitution was quickly published. The object was stated bluntly to be 'the re-establishment of the Independence of Ireland'. The means of achieving this were set as 'the training of the youth of Ireland, mentally and physically, by teaching them scouting and military exercises, Irish history and the Irish language'. The real motive as stated was to get the boys of Ireland in their extreme youth and train them as patriot soldiers and prospective leaders of the next generation. The Fianna was, in effect, a cadet corps for a future revolutionary army. When the Fianna was formed that army did not exist. It was to come into existence far sooner than anyone then hoped. And the Fianna was to take its rightful place in its ranks.

The named Fianna Éireann was in itself a happy choice. It was the third great comradeship to bear the honoured name.

There was the first Fianna, the Fianna of the second century,

175

Ireland's original regular army. Not alone a well-trained well-disciplined army, but one of the world's great orders of knighthood. No wonder that admission to the Fianna was regarded as the highest honour in ancient Ireland, that expulsion from its ranks was the greatest disgrace.

But the first Fianna passed away and Ireland entered upon her long period of suffering. The foreigner came in and stayed in. Generation after generation rose in arms in heroic but vain efforts to regain their country's freedom. History tells how they fought and failed, and in failing handed on the torch of liberty to their sons, right down to our own times.

Then in the middle of the last century the honoured name of Fianna Éireann was resurrected. A handful of young men decided to strike again, to strike with a secret army this time. And they gave their new army the name of the Fenian Brotherhood to show that their movement was based on the age-old ideals of patriotism and valour and comradeship of the ancient Fianna.

Like so many other great movements this too failed, but as often happened before, proved more glorious in defeat than in victory. Beaten in the field, thousands of the Fenians were flung into prisons or transported overseas. Many died in their living tombs, many others broke down in body and mind, but those who survived suffered proudly on. And outside, their remaining comrades proved their right to the proud name of the Fianna.

Facing the might of an empire they snatched their suffering comrades out of the prison van in the English city and died on the scaffold with the proud prayer 'God Save Ireland' on their lips. They blew down the walls and burst open gates of English jails in daring efforts to free their fellow soldiers. They sailed across the world and carried their brother Fenians out of Australian convict settlements under the very guns of the guarding warships.

The world had sneered at these Fenians in defeat, now it thrilled to the daring of their exploits and these were the traditions handed down to the boys of the third Fianna back in 1909 when 'Madam' and her colleagues chose that ancient name for their young organisation.

Pádraig Pearse himself summed it up in these words: 'The Fianna of today are the third heroic comradeship that has borne that name. The first Fianna, the Fianna of Fionn, have been dead for nearly 2,000 years. A few old grey-haired men, the veterans of the second Fianna, are with us still. The lads of the third Fianna, the familiar green-shirted, bare-kneed young soldiers who have prepared the way for our Irish Volunteers inherit the gallant name and tradition of the ancient Fianna and the mighty purpose of the modern Fenians. Were ever boys heirs to such a great inheritance?'

Early Days of the Fianna

And it was in this spirit that the boy soldiers of the third Fianna settled down to work. What did this work consist of? In its own youthful way it was as extensive as the training of the modern soldier. The boys learned foot drill, arms drill, scouting, signalling, first aid, fieldcraft, campcraft and a host of other fascinating subjects for impressionable young warriors of twelve to twenty-four.

Mental training was stressed at least as hard as purely military training. The boys were taught to stand up for right at all costs, that lying was not alone dishonourable but downright stupid, that they were to be clean in body and mind, that they should be courteous to women and children, the old and infirm. The movement was strictly non-sectarian but the Fheinnidhe were taught to be reverent and faithful to their religion, to respect the convictions of others, but never to deny their own. It all sounds nearly priggish now, but there was nothing priggish about it to these boy soldiers.

The strong national background to all training probably helped in this. For the first time in their lives the boys really learned Irish history, real living history, not a dry collection of dates and names. To their amazement they found they belonged to an ancient nation with a culture and tradition of its own. They revelled in the stories and songs of the old Gaelic warriors, and in the great deeds of later days. These they never heard of in the schools of those days and so they were trained for their tasks in the Ireland of the future.

Judged by modern standards the training facilities were laughable. An old barn, the use once a week of a Gaelic League or parish hall, a back room in someone's house, a shed in a yard, even a cellar in a tenement. Such were the 'barracks' of a Fianna unit. But youthful enthusiasm laughed at such handicaps.

Saturdays and Sundays the open country was their training ground if the weather was anyway possible. And in the summer the joys of the weekend or longer camps. Camp gear was as up-to-date as everything else. Battered old sewed bell tents, an odd homemade affair of the 'bivvy' variety, a bit of tarpaulin against a hedge. But it taught them to take care of themselves.

Organisation was equally simple. The smallest unit was the squad of about six boys commanded by a veteran of fourteen to sixteen, two squads made a section, two or more squads a troop or sluagh under a lieutenant or captain, generally a grey-beard of eighteen to twenty summers. In large centres the various slughtaí [*sic*] in an area were administered by a district council, and the entire movement was governed by a central council sitting in Dublin under the chairmanship of the chief scout. Later on companies and battalions and even brigades were formed, but in the beginning the Fianna was organised on the simple lines set out, and very well it worked.

Many an old soldier of today first learned what it meant to take pride in his uniform as an awkward Fianna boy. Quite a snappy outfit it was. A green double-breasted shirt with brass buttons, and the usual scout hat, also in green, fastened up on the right side. This was supposed to help them to shoot, rather an ironical touch in a force that first carried out arms drill with hurleys. But the guns too came along in time.

Like the modern army, the Fianna had its colours and its specialist and rank badges. Its flag was appropriately based on the old battle standard of the ancient Fianna – a gold sunburst on a blue ground. There were three classes of Fheinnidhe, each of which wore its own distinctive insignia in the shape of coloured whistle cords on the left shoulder. For example a 3rd class Fheinnidhe wore a green cord, 2nd class a white cord, and 1st class a green white and orange plaited cord. This was probably the first occasion the tricolour was used since Thomas Francis Meagher introduced it in 1848.

Rank badges were equally simple. A squad leader bore saffron epaulettes, a section leader red, a lieutenant blue and a captain blue with a white bar. In those early days Captain was the highest rank.

The Fianna had also its own motto, the proud centuries old slogan of the ancient Fianna: 'With truth on our lips, strength in out arms, and purity in our hearts we come safe out of every danger.' It sounds a bit high-flown in these cynical times, but it was taken very seriously in those brave young days.

Such was the Fianna in those early years from 1909 to 1913. There was no question of the new movement sweeping the country like the proverbial prairie fire, but it did make steady progress. Starting in the cities, Dublin, Cork, Limerick, Galway, the green-shirted young soldiers slowly but surely became a familiar sight throughout the country. But no one took the movement very seriously except possibly the boys themselves and their leaders.

Foundation of the Volunteers

Then things began to happen. It looked as if the long promised Home Rule Act was to pass the British House of Commons. The Ulster Orangemen began a strong agitation against it. They were supported by an influential element among British politicians, were lavishly financed, and had the active sympathy of a section at least of the British army. They planned to set up an Ulster Provisional Government and oppose Home Rule by force of arms. With this end in view the Ulster Volunteer Force was organised.

The nationalists all over Ireland promptly replied in kind, and in 1913 the Irish Volunteers were formed. Unlike the Fianna initially, the new force did literally sweep the country like a prairie fire.

And now the wisdom of the founders of the Fianna was proved. The main problem confronting the new Volunteer army was the provision of officers and instructors. A number of ex-British soldiers did come forward and did Trojan work. But naturally the bulk of such people would not look favourably upon such a movement. This applied particularly to the ex-officer class. But another source was available. By 1913 the early Fianna recruits had reached military age. Whenever a Fianna sluagh existed these older lads were transferred to the Volunteers as instructors, and many of them became officers. Three members of the Fianna central council were appointed to the Volunteer Executive. One of these was Liam Mellows, another Seán Heuston who was to die two years later before a British firing squad. The Fianna had met its first big test, the job for which it was formed, and was not found wanting. When the need arose it was ready and stepped into the gap. If this was its solitary achievement the Boy army had fully justified itself. But its record of service to Ireland was in reality only beginning.

The Howth gun-running

The Fianna closed up its ranks and went on with its work of training more soldiers for the future. The older boys stepped into the place of their comrades who had passed over to the Volunteers and carried on.

The Fianna very soon came into the limelight again. In July 1914, a big cargo of rifles and ammunition was run into Howth, County Dublin, on the late Erskine Childers' yacht. The Dublin Brigade, Irish Volunteers marched out to received the arms. A picked Fianna detachment accompanied the Volunteers with a trek cart, a sort of oversize machine gun 'pram'. They had the special task of transporting the ammunition.

The cargo collected, the march back to Dublin commenced. At Clontarf a couple of companies of the King's Own Scottish Borderers and some hundred police barred the way. The British officer in charge demanded the rifles, the Volunteers of course refused. An attempt to seize them was beaten off with rifle butts. The Volunteers clamoured for ammunition and some officers and issued strict orders that no ammunition was to be issued. The men were far too raw to tackle regular troops at this time. It is doubtful if many of them could even have loaded their rifles if they had ammunition.

The Fianna stood firm. Armed with heavy batons they refused to weaken. Not a round of ammunition was issued. Eventually the Volunteers slipped off across country with their riffles, and the precious ammunition was transported to safety by motor. If these lads had wavered for a moment the ball ammunition had got into the hands of the then half-disciplined and semi-trained Volunteers, the results would have been disaster. The bloodless victory of Clontarf would have been turned into a bloody massacre. It would almost certainly have meant the end of that great Volunteer force which was later to win independence for the greater part of our country. Again the Fianna had made good.

The Fianna in Easter Week

Events now moved rapidly. A few days after the gun-running the First World War broke out. In the clash of millions of armed men abroad, the troubles of Ireland were forgotten by the world for the time being. The long promised Home Rule Bill was shelved 'for the duration' – for ever, as it turned out. Appeals were issued to young Irishmen to go off to fight 'for the freedom of small nations'. Thousands of Volunteers answered this call.

But those left behind closed up the ranks, they held their job was to win freedom for their own small nation. For two years more preparations continued apace, and the Fianna kept on transferring its older boys to the Volunteers and filling the gaps with their younger brothers.

History records how the Volunteers struck on Easter Monday, 1916, and proclaimed the Republic. The Fianna's part in this great protest in arms was in keeping with its ideals and traditions. Every Republican post had its detachment of Fianna boys. They acted as scouts, orderlies, runners and despatch riders. Two of them were killed in action trying to get their despatches through – Seán Howard and Joe Healy. Two Fianna officers were shot by sentence of British courtmartial after the Rising, Captain Seán Heuston and Captain Con Colbert. Commandant Liam Mellows commanded the Volunteers in Galway and escaped to America after the Rising. The chief of the Fianna, Countess Markievicz, was second in command in the Stephen's Green area and was sentenced to imprisonment for life. One of the more spectacular tasks of the entire Rising was carried out by the Fianna. A special detachment of them, under Captain (later Major General) Pádraig Ó Dálaigh, had the honour to be detailed to capture and destroy the magazine fort. They gained admission to the fort by a ruse, rushed and disarmed the guard, set fire to the ammunition stores, and retreated successfully and joined the Four Courts garrison.

The Fianna had faced its second great test, and once again it was not found wanting.

After the Rising

At the time the Easter Rising was regarded as a crushing military defeat. The great Volunteer organisation, built up so patiently, was apparently destroyed. Its leaders were dead or in prison, the bulk of its rank and file in internment camps. Perhaps it was due to their training that the Fianna seemed to be the first to recover from the stupor of despair – for that is really what it was. It is a matter of historical fact that within one month of the collapsed Rising, all available Fianna officers who were alive or at liberty met in Dublin to consider the situation.

It was a black look-out. It seemed as if another generation had failed. So it was calmly decided to start all over again, to go back to the original object of the Fianna, to train the boys of Ireland to receive the fight in the next generation. But events moved quicker than that. By 1917 the Volunteers as well as the Fianna were re-organised, by 1918 the entire revolutionary movement – political as well as military – was stronger than ever. A resurgent nation was on the march.

Then arose another crisis, with a special interest for the Fianna, the conscription menace. In 1918 the British government decided to extend the conscription of Ireland. The result was amazing. In tens of thousands the young men of the country flocked into the Volunteers, clamouring to be trained to meet this new threat. Companies grew to battalions overnight, battalions to brigades. Again the call went out for instructors and again the Fianna stepped into the gap. Not alone officers and older lads, but any urchin with training, and these boys stood no nonsense, they knew their jobs and they did it. The threat to impose conscription was dropped, and Volunteers and Fianna settled down again to prepare for the 'next round'.

It was not long coming. In 1918 the Sinn Féin or Republican Party was returned to power by an overwhelming majority. It set up the Dáil in Dublin and established a Republican government. This government took over the Volunteers as the Irish Republican Army, and the Fianna became a recognised corps of this army, its official training corps. It did not mean much change for the Fianna but it did give it official recognition and financial backing.

The Resumption of Hostilities

In due course the Dáil was proclaimed, fruitless efforts were made to suppress it and all its institutions, including, of course, the IRA. The army was ordered to hit back, active fighting opened in 1919 and reached its peak in 1920–21.

In hundreds the Fianna kept pouring trained recruits into the ranks of the Volunteers. It also carried out much of the scouting and intelligence and communications work. The Republican communication service composed of whole-time despatch riders – the forerunner of the modern signal corps – was recruited almost exclusively from the Fianna. In some areas special Fianna active service units composed of Officers, NCOs were formed, in others the older Fheinnidhe fought with Volunteer columns.

In this manner the Fianna, in addition to providing the Volunteers with their trained recruits and carrying out all sorts of special duties, took more than their share in the active fighting. Many of them made the supreme sacrifice, in action, on the scaffold, before the firing squads. Many others were captured and thrown into prison or internment camps. But like their elder brothers in the Volunteers, they never faltered until the end came.

The Truce and After

And it came at last in 1921. In July that year a truce or armistice was agreed upon between the Irish and British armies. In the following

December a treaty of peace was signed, which excluded temporarily it was hoped – six counties of Ulster. It looked at last as if the long struggle was over, that peace with honour had come to Ireland for few thought that partition could last for more than a year or so.

But it was not to be. The government and the Dáil disagreed on the peace terms, the split spread to the Republican army, and almost before anyone could realise what had happened Ireland was plunged into war again, into the horror of Civil War this time.

The Fianna suffered like all other organisations. Many of its officers and boys in disgust remained neutral, others joined the new regular army, others again the Republican forces. History was repeating itself with a vengeance. The ancient Fianna of Fionn MacCumhaill went down to disaster in the welter of civil strife. And in the bitter years of 1922-23 there died another great heroic comradeship.

So ends the story of the third Fianna. It is hoped that it will help the readers to realise what this corps of boy soldiers did to make Ireland of today possible. In this way it may serve as a small tribute to old comrades, living or dead, with whom so many of us first learned our soldiering. It was due to them that we of today do not have to lament with Oisín:

> *All the Fianna have passed away,*
> *There remains to them no heir.*

The Fianna may have passed away, but their heirs serve on in the ranks of every army and LDF unit in the Ireland of today.

APPENDICES

Colonel (later Lieutenant-General) M.J. Costello's work in establishing *An Cosantóir* represented only a tiny part of his efforts in the cause of the defence of the nation during the emergency years.

Born in Cloughjordan, County Tipperary in 1904, Costello joined the old IRA after the arrest of his father and served in the War of Independence as the very capable intelligence officer of the Tipperary No. 1 Brigade. In 1922 he joined the National army and was promoted to colonel-commandant at a very young age by General Michael Collins; after the outbreak of the Civil War, Costello had proved himself to be a staff officer of outstanding ability and had showed great courage under fire.

Collins' high opinion of the young Costello's abilities were later shared by the US Army. In 1927 Costello graduated from the US army command and staff course at Fort Leavenworth with distinction and was recommended for the even more prestigious War College, then being attended by Major Dwight Eisenhower. His talents were needed at home however, where he played a pivotal role in establishing the Irish Military College.

In 1940, Colonel Costello was appointed O/C Southern Command and as such bore primary responsibility for the defence of the south coast of Ireland, considered the most likely route for invasion.

The additional material provided in these appendices give Costello's informed opinions on such topics as the Blitzkrieg warfare with which the Germans had overrun western Europe, or guerrilla warfare which was regarded as a defence option in the event of Ireland being attacked by superior forces.

GUERRILLA WARFARE

by Colonel M.J. Costello

Introduction

A great many members of the army and the LSF are experienced guerrilla fighters. Many valuable lessons from the past are being made generally available through the historical articles appearing in *An Cosantóir*. If this experience and these lessons are to be usefully applied to present conditions the vast difference between the conditions of the past and the probable conditions of any guerrilla fighting which we may have to undertake in future must be clearly understood.

Developments in aircraft, armoured fighting vehicles, wireless, and other weapons of war will change the nature of the fighting.

A much greater change will be due to the improvement in the discipline, training and armament of the guerrillas who it will be possible for us to put in the field.

But the greatest change of all arises from the fact that guerrilla warfare will be only one part of our resistance to any invader. If we have to undertake guerrilla operations in defence of Ireland these operations will only be a secondary phase of that defence. We will endeavour to prevent invasion, to drive out any invader, to hold the invader and if he should succeed in advancing we will contest that advance yard by yard and make him pay a heavy price for every sod which he may gain. Our guerrilla operations of the future would be undertaken not as they were in 1920–21 as our only armed resistance but as a support and a supplement to the resistance of regular military formations.

Guerrilla operations so conducted in co-ordination with the operations of a regular army and naturally much more effective that the unsupported efforts of guerrillas.

There is a good historical precedent for this situation of a guerrilla welfare waged in conjunction with regular military operations. The turning point in Napoleon's career was his attempted conquest of Spain and Portugal. This war has passed into history as the 'Spanish Ulcer' – the running-sore which drained away the strength of the great French Emperor and his hitherto invincible armies. The Spaniards waged a relentless guerrilla warfare while the British army under Wellington fought a series of regular campaigns. The French would have disposed of either enemy in a short time. Relative to the French, the Spaniards were very poor in quality and the British army was very small. The combination of Spanish guerrillas and British regulars proved invincible.

In studying the guerrilla operations of the past we should therefore attempt to visualise the conditions of future. We should ask ourselves in every case how bombers, tanks, mortars, wireless and a multiplicity of light machine guns would strengthen the enemy. We should consider how the better equipment available to us today would affect the issue. We should remember that the ambush or raid of the future will be carried out against the background of a larger and a continuous conflict and that the guerrilla of the future if unfortunately he should be called into being will have powerful military support while his predecessor of 1920–21 had to rely upon his own unit.

Definition

Guerrilla warfare may be defined as the fight kept up in territory occupied by the enemy. The conditions in such territory may vary a great deal. The population may be left in their homes and the ordinary life of the country may go on as it did Ireland in 1920–1921. On the other hand, the country may be devastated, as were parts of the Boer Republics during the South Africa war. The extent and strength of enemy occupation will depend upon the conduct of the war by the guerrillas; the more active and successful they are, the greater the number of garrisons required by the enemy and the stronger must each of these garrisons be. The nature of the war will also depend upon the extent to which the guerrillas are supported by regular troops operating elsewhere in the theatre of operations.

General Nature of Guerrilla War

The whole object of the guerrillas is to inflict as much loss and damage as possible upon the enemy while at the same time avoiding anything in the nature of a fight to a finish and preventing the enemy from pinning them down. Guerrilla warfare is largely one of evasion but it is not warfare at all unless it is characterised by a ceaseless and relentless offensive against the weak points of the enemy.

Advantages of Guerrillas

The main advantages of well-trained guerrillas are:

a)   their elusiveness
b)   their mobility
c)   their accurate information

In order to turn these advantages to account, they must have no impediments, no vulnerable lines of communications, and they must be able to march faster and farther than their enemies. From the nature of things, they will have an intimate knowledge of the country; and the entire population will be their eyes and ears. The very highest standard of physical fitness and stamina must be developed They must constantly be on the move, constantly studying the enemy dispositions, and always ready to pounce like a hawk on any quarry that appears within their reach. Only the very best and fittest of our young men will be fit for such operations and these must constantly improve their physical powers by exercise and sports, such as cross-country running.

Use of Cover and Obstacles

With their detailed knowledge of the country, guerrillas will be able to retire to and move through areas in which it will be difficult for the enemy to follow them rapidly. Passes through bogs and mountains which can be used by them may not be known to the enemy or may be so difficult that he will be unable to use them. In difficult country the enemy's superiority in heavy weapons will be of no use to him since he must be as light and mobile as the guerrillas if he is to move quickly. Indeed, the advantage will probably be with the local troops, who will be spared the task of carrying large amounts of small arms ammunition, grenades and mines. These should be available to them in secret dumps in different areas.

A retreat through a defile will provide an opportunity of holding off superior numbers, at least until nightfall. It will provide opportunities for ambushes and even for leading the enemy into a trap from which he cannot escape. The systematic destruction of roads and railways is an essential feature of operations. These must be destroyed again immediately they are repaired.

Keep the Initiative

It is essential in guerrilla warfare to keep the initiative. If such forces allow themselves to be kept continuously on the run, the natural advantages of the guerrilla will be lost and even the most excellent physical and moral stamina will not stand the strain. In order to keep the initiative, they must constantly strike back and continually develop new threats and new tactics. The one sure way to prevent the enemy from keeping guerrilla forces on the run is for them to give him no rest.

Objectives of Guerrillas

Guerrillas must neglect no chance of striking a blow and they must by various ruses, create opportunities of action. The nature of these ruses is not a proper subject for public discussion, but they are well known to the many experienced guerrilla fighters who are available. The most natural objective is the enemy's lines of communication. Attacks on convoys, depots or bases should yield rich booty and they will tend to paralyse enemy movements.

At all costs, the enemy must be prevented from moving in small parties. Every small party must be snapped up without delay. Large units are easy to locate and easy to follow and the enemy will have serious difficulties in supplying them.

A constant watch should be kept on enemy garrisons and every movement of the enemy should be at least sniped if not more seriously harassed. His troops should be kept under arms every night by sniping attacks or raids. If he grows accustomed to these and relaxes his vigilance, opportunity for a larger operation will occur. A garrison continuously sniped and worried may, in time, be surprised and wiped out if it does not remain always on the alert. The morale of the enemy will not long survive the continuous watchfulness and the continuous pin-pricking which guerrillas can impose.

An attempted round up, or any other form of cordon, by enemy troops offers an objective, which must not be missed. If any of our troops are inside the cordon, it is imperative that it be attacked from outside, i.e. from the rear. Well-trained guerrillas, competently led, have nothing to fear from a cordon of less strength than about five hundred men per mile. Hit without delay, hit hard, and hit as many separate points on the cordon as is possible. The forces surrounded by the cordon will then have no difficulty in punching a hole in a weak part of the cordon and escaping.

Even without assistance from outside the cordon, the units surrounded can escape, given skilful, resolute and inspiring leadership. The history of the Boer War, the Spanish Peninsular War and the American Civil War all afford examples of how the cordon can effectively be met. The classic example, however, is nearer to us. It is the fight of the 3rd Cork Brigade column at Crossbarry. The writer has come across no fight which affords a better or more inspiring example than that of Barry's column.

The plans for a breakthrough of a cordon should be based upon a careful consideration of the ground so as to make the most of obstacles. Good timing is also necessary. The enemy must not be allowed to close in too much, as the smaller the circle becomes, the stronger it becomes, and the more readily can it be reinforced at the point of attack.

Timing is also important because feints and distracting operations from outside the cordon should be co-ordinated with the breakthrough. Should it be possible to defer a breakthrough until nightfall, the get-away can be made under cover of darkness with greatly improved chances of success. The breakthrough must not, however, be delayed too long. The Boer army, under Cronje, was lost at Paardeberg because he did not break out in time. He stuck to his wagons and held his head to the ground passively, with the result that he lost his men as well as his wagons.

The get-away must be rapid so as to ensure against being pinned down. In this, as in every phase of operations, greater mobility than that of the enemy is essential to the guerrillas. Our columns in 1919–21 had this because they were young and in the pink of condition and because they travelled light.

The enemy must not be allowed to concentrate upon one part of the country and to mop it up while remaining on the defensive elsewhere. While enemy concentrations should be harassed, the immediate and principal action of the guerrillas should be to intensify operations elsewhere. This policy is necessary because they must seize the opportunities of bolder action presented by the withdrawal of mobile enemy forces for the purpose of the concentration. Every weakening of his forces in an area creates an opportunity for the concentration of guerrilla forces in that area. The only means open to the guerrillas to relieve pressure on a hard-pressed area is to draw off the enemy by hitting him hard elsewhere. The effect upon the enemy of an outbreak of activity in any area other than that upon which he is concentrating, is damaging from every point of view. It makes the concentration seem foolish and distracts his attention from the job in hand.

Guerrillas must be prepared to meet and defeat an attempt to cordon off the country into sectors by occupied lines of blockhouses. The British lines of barbed wire and blockhouses in South Africa were a great factor in the defeat of the Boers. It would seem at first sight that in this country it would be much easier for an enemy to create effective cordons owing to the very much smaller area of our territory. In fact, the smaller area of Ireland is offset by the vastly greater amount of cover for guerrillas and especially by the broken nature of the country which will reduce the mobility of the enemy, provided we properly exploit it by belts of demolitions. In South Africa the British eventually attained a degree of mobility as high, if not higher than the Boers. This was decisive as it enabled them to concentrate rapidly and even if the Boers did break through a line of blockhouses, they were likely to meet a British column immediately they did so. In this close country, by making it impassable for wheeled transport, guerrilla forces could and should be more mobile than any enemy.

Lines of blockhouses should be opposed from the first. Guerrilla forces should fight against their erection. If the lines are built in spite of them, they must be broken through frequently and constantly harassed. If they cannot be broken through by day, they can almost certainly be passed by night. The garrisons present objectives for surprise attacks. Mortars, grenades, mines and flame-throwers can all be used effectively. The difficulty experienced in capturing RIC barracks has taught us to value the weapons now in our possession and experience of these attacks with inadequate means should surely be fruitful in the better circumstances of the present.

Night Operations

On account of their intimate knowledge of the country, night operations should be much easier for guerrilla troops than for an invader. At night, the bayonet, the grenade, the mine, the shot-gun, the rifle and the revolver are the only weapons which can be used effectively, and since guerrilla forces should be able to use these at least as well as an enemy they should be not only equal but much superior to him at night, counting man for man.

Mobility

Several references have already been made to mobility but too much emphasis cannot be laid upon its importance. Guerrilla forces MUST BE more mobile than the enemy. They must increase their mobility by every means and lose no chance nor neglect any means of lessening his.

The first condition of high mobility is the physical fitness of the troops. This must be developed and maintained by every means. Attention to health an hygiene must be unremitting. Men should have the best possible clothing and they should be well fed, not necessarily with the soft foods to which people have now become accustomed. Oatmeal, milk and potatoes sustained the physical flower of our race in the past and can do so again. Meat and vegetables should also be available.

Bicycles are the most suitable means of transport and they should be available in each local area in sufficient numbers and in good condition. Bicycles cannot, of course, be used in bogs and mountains and they must therefore be preserved in carefully concealed dumps, adjacent to such areas. Men must be trained to march and cycle as far and as fast as possible.

The mobility of the enemy must first of all be reduced by thoroughly and systematically destroying roads in accordance with plans already prepared. Anti-tank obstacles should be created in critical areas in which the terrain is suitable for the work. All motor vehicles, bicycles and petrol should be denied to the enemy by removal or destruction. By retiring into territory in which use can be made of difficult or little known routes the mobility of guerrilla forces can be made relatively still greater than that of the enemy. No enemy should be able to cross a bog with the same speed and safety as these light troops. Even though our rivers are not great obstacles they can be used to advantage. Local guerrillas should easily be able to arrange to cross with speed and safety in boats, rafts, flying ferries or over little known fords. The enemy, if he is travelling light, will take an appreciable time to follow up if the means of crossing are hidden or destroyed.

Intelligence

Just as guerrillas must constantly strive to be more mobile than the enemy, they must make the most of their advantages in the matter of intelligence. They must strain every nerve to organise a most perfect system and to disorganise and frustrate the intelligence services of the enemy. It was in this more than in any other aspect of guerrilla warfare that the pre-truce IRA excelled. Every man must be made to realise the importance of the work and to pass on rapidly every item of information he gets, no matter how trivial it may seem to him. Every man must equally be taught how to frustrate the enemy intelligence. There can be no relaxation to this work. Constant vigilance is necessary. Intelligence needs the active and trained assistance of every soldier and every member of the LSF. It is only when surprised that guerrillas can be beaten. A good intelligence service is as essential as strict security measures to prevent surprise.

Mobilisation and Concentration

While guerrillas must be concentrated to fight major actions they will normally be dispersed in smaller fighting units of varying strengths. This dispersion is necessary so that they may be always on the spot to snap up enemy scouts and small parties of every kind, so that they may constantly harass enemy posts, so that they may keep roads blocked as quickly as they are repaired, so that difficulties of supply may be overcome so as to avoid danger of the enemy scoring a real success by pouncing upon a large body and so as to maintain the system of intelligence and inter-communication. Arrangements for mobilisation and concentration must, therefore, be thoroughly worked out and frequently rehearsed in peace-times.

Communications

Intelligence, mobilisation, concentration and the control of operations depend upon the working of a quick and dependable communication system. The mainstay of the system will be cyclist or motor-cyclist despatch riders, horsemen and relays of runners on foot. Radio can be used to some extent. Visual signalling by lamp or flag, signal fires and, in some areas, telephones and telegraphs can and should be used, but none of these can be depended upon.

Supply

Supplies must be available in dumps carefully concealed and well placed with reference to likely areas of operations and to hide-outs in difficult districts. These dumps must, however, be looked upon as reserves and guerrillas should rely above everything else upon living off the enemy, not only in the matter of armament but in the matter of food and clothing other than uniform.

Past Experience and Present Conditions

While the fullest use should be made of past experience, it should be fully realised that as mentioned in the introductory paragraphs conditions in any guerrilla fight which we may have to wage in future will be very different from those of the past. The most obvious minor difference is that, in future, guerrillas will fight in uniform. The facility of appearing as inoffensive citizens which was enjoyed by many of the IRA in the past will be denied.

It is to be expected that the enemy will be more numerous, more skilful, better led and more ruthless than the British army of 1920–21. A more systematic and thorough-going offensive by any future enemy may be anticipated.

An invader will, in future, secure more information for air reconnaissance despite the best efforts at concealment.

In all, or almost all, other respects our position in guerrilla fighting in the next war would be vastly better than in the last if we make the most of our opportunities, both in preparation and during the fight.

Our guerrilla forces will be better armed. The RIC barracks which was a fortress to us long ago would stand no chance against the weapons now available. We are better trained and can achieve an even higher standard of training. We are better organised and have every facility for perfecting our organisation. We are better disciplined and this, too, can be perfected.

Instead of a sporadic struggle fought independently in local areas, we can stage a systematic, co-ordinated offensive all over the country.

We shall not make the mistake of the Boers who did not embark upon guerrilla operations until their main armies were beaten out of the field. Neither will we fall into the opposite error of failing to make full use of our strength from the very outset to smash any invasion.

A NEW TYPE OF WARFARE?
GERMAN STRATEGY AND TACTICS

by Colonel M.J. Costello

Of all the tasks which confront us, the most important is clear thinking.
M. Reynaud, Prime Minister of France, 21 May 1940

Seldom since history began have there been victories so complete and so far-reaching in their effects as those won by the German army and air force in the present war. Never before have such victories been so rapidly won. It is natural, therefore, that there should be much speculation about the reasons for these tremendous events.

The peoples of the vanquished and the neutral states were astounded and the neutral press devoted much space to the 'secrets' of the German successes. It is, of course, impossible to write the history of these swift campaigns or to analyse properly the cause of victory and defeat. The material upon which the historian or the critic must base his conclusions is not available and will not be available for, perhaps, a generation, if, indeed, it is ever fully available. It is, however, possible to examine in the light of known facts some of the opinions and excuses which have been published in explanation of these world-shaking events. It is necessary for us to do this now, even with the meagre information at our disposal, because a wrong and dangerous impression has been created in the public mind and because even the smallest scrap of information on the questions involved deserves to be closely studied by those who are devoting themselves to the defence of their country. Such preparation demands that we look into the future and endeavour to meet every possible variety of assault upon us from any quarter whatsoever.

Alleged New Tactics

The impression has been created that Germany won her victories by new methods of warfare and it has been widely stated that the attack with modern means is stronger than the defence. No evidence which would support either assertion has come under the notice of the writer. On the contrary, those methods which are described as new were well known in theory or practice for many years. And before it is accepted that these methods are invincible, it must be shown that all possible counter-measures have been tried in vain. There is no reason for any soldier who was a student of his profession and who was aware of the published facts about the combat power of the combatants to be astonished at the results of the campaigns of 1940. There are, in fact, many military prophets who can have the doubtful satisfaction of saying to their countrymen 'I told you so'. The admirable but not original sentiment of M. Reynaud, which stands at the head of this article, is taken from the following:

> The truth is that our classic conception of the conduct of war has come up against a new conception. At the basis of this conception there is not only the massive use of heavy armoured divisions or co-operation between them and aeroplanes, but the

creation of disorder in the enemy's rear by means of parachute raids, which in Holland nearly caused the fall of the Hague, and in Belgium seized the strongest fort of Liege.

I will not speak to you of the false news and the orders given by means of the telephone to the civil authorities with the object, for example, of causing hurried evacuations.

You will understand that of all the tasks which confront us, the most important is clear thinking. We must think of new type of warfare which we are facing and take immediate decisions.

M. Reynaud, 21-5-40

Tom Wintringham's excellent book *New Ways of Warfare* attributes the German victories to the same methods and also to their tactics of infiltration in attack for which he says the Allies were not prepared. The consensus of the views published is that these 'new methods' account for the rapid downfall of Poland, Norway, Holland, Belgium and France.

These methods are:

1. The employment of aircraft in masses to attack ground troops with bomb and bullet.

2. The employment of a masses (divisions) of armoured fighting vehicles moving fast and far to the rear of the battle front.

3. The attack of vital points by parachutists.

4. Sabotage and attacks on civilian morale, including the activities of fifth columnists, spreading of false information and the issue of false orders to enemy troops.

5. The tactical method of attack called 'infiltration'.

The Attack from the Air

The attacks by dive-bombers and other low-flying aircraft are said to have had a decisive effect on the fighting but their success is said to have been due more to the moral effect of the attacks than to the material results in casualties, etc. It is easy to believe these statements. Since the Allies were not equipped or trained to make similar mass attacks upon the Germans, it is probable that their armies were mentally unprepared for the terrible and nerve-racking onslaught. The moral effect of surprise, of the unexpected and the unknown, was therefore, added to the serious material results. The importance of this moral effect is indirectly illustrated by the fact that the withdrawal from Dunkirk was successfully carried out. This in any circumstances would have been one of the most difficult operations of war. It would have been quite impossible if the troops involved had not nerved themselves to stand up to dive-bombing. They had presumably got used to it by that time and the moral effect of surprise had worn off. (That the force of the initial German air attack had at this time been somewhat spent was probably of less consequence.) The civilian populations of great English cities have withstood similar hammerings from the air and it would be impossible for any human beings to do so if they had not visualised the menace in advance and been mentally prepared for it.

It is not true to say that the German employment of massed aircraft in battle is new. This method of attack was developed during the last war and employed with striking successes by both the Germans and the British. Ludendorff, who was what we would call the chief of staff of the German armies, issued a memorandum in February 1918, containing the following:

The employment of low-flying aeroplanes on the battlefield, and their co-operation in the fighting on the ground, by opening machine-gun fire or attacking with bombs and hand grenades, is particularly effective from the point of view of morale, both on our own and the enemy's troops. The systematic participation in the battle of massed flying formations (battle flights) against ground targets is of extreme importance. In the attack, battle airplanes fly ahead of and carry the infantry along with them, keeping down the fire of the enemy's infantry and barrage batteries. In the defence, the appearance of battle aeroplanes affords visible proof to heavily engaged troops that the higher command is in close touch with the front, and is employing every possible means to support the fighting troops. Confidence in a successful defence is thereby strengthened. The object of the battle flights is to shatter the enemy's nerve by repeated attacks in close formation and thus to obtain a decisive influence on the course of the fighting. They cause confusion to a considerable distance behind the enemy's front line, dislocate traffic and inflict appreciable losses on re-inforcements hastening up to the battlefield. In the battle flights, the higher command possesses powerful weapons which would be employed at the decisive point of the attack ...

Commencing on 21 March 1918, there began one of the three most significant battles of the last Great War in France. In this battle the German armies broke through the British front and for a day separated the British and French. One of the biggest single factors in stopping the German advance was the success of the attacks made by the British Royal Air Force on advancing German columns. In the Battle of Amiens, which began on 8 August 1918, and marked the beginning of the end for the German armies, the employment by the British of aircraft against ground troops was an important factor.

America, after the war, classified her military aircraft into bombardment, reconnaissance, pursuit and attack. The latter category consisted of units organised for the specific purpose of attacks on ground troops and was equipped with machines specially designed for this purpose. From the time that the German air force appeared in the open, and during all the years up to the outbreak of the present war, it was no secret that the Germans were paying particular attention to preparation for the intervention on the battlefield of a powerful aviation equipped especially with dive-bombers.

In recent years the British army adopted a Swedish gun for the purpose of defence against the diving or low-flying attack. Whether this gun existed in adequate numbers, whether it was suitable for its purposes, the writer does not know but it is evident that Britain's Allies were not adequately equipped to meet this menace and, what is even more important, the troops of none of the Allies seem to have been mentally prepared. They were surprised by a method of attack twenty-two years old and developed in intensity to correspond to the improvement in aircraft which has taken place during these twenty-two years.

Is there an answer to the dive-bomber? This is the practical question of the moment. The perfect answer is obviously to have such air superiority as to drive them out the air. But where this answer is not possible, the menace can still be met by full education of everyone so that such attacks will not be a surprise and so that the moral effect will be no greater than the material results justify. Everyone liable to attack, and that is every person in the land, should know that the noise won't kill them, that the noise is meant to terrify and that if we refuse to be terrified this weapon loses a lot of the power which it wielded in Europe last year; that is to say, if we have a sufficiently high standard of morale, not alone in the army by among the civil population, we can 'take it' without disastrous results.

It should be fully understood that the dive-bomber has poor chance of hitting a small target. Even big bridges and large ships are missed more often than they are hit. It is also important to remember that the second or third or even the hundredth bomb has no better chance of hitting the target than the first one. Whereas artillery and mortar fire increases in accuracy with every observed shot, in the case of the bomber every shot is a first shot from a new position.

With a full appreciation of the potentialities of attack from the air, we can minimise its effect by suitable defensive measures. The most important of these, as far as the army and LDF are concerned, are, mental preparation and development of morale, concealment so that the enemy has no target to aim at, dispersion so that even if he sees a target it be small and of little value, and the use of slit trenches and other works which will protect us from everything except a direct hit. By these means we can lessen the effect of dive-bombing to such and extent as to defeat its purpose.

The Attack by Means of Armoured Fighting Vehicles

It is hard to understand how the idea got about that Germany devised a new method of war when she created her now famous 'Panzer' divisions and employed them to sweep completely around some of the Allied armies and in every case to penetrate far to the rear of the enemy, disrupting and paralysing communication, supply and the movement of reserves. These fast-moving units consist of tanks of varying size and power, of armoured cars, motor-cyclists and of infantry carried in lorries. The German army had its first lesson in the employment of masses of tanks in 1917. At the Battle of Cambrai in November of that year, the British won a spectacular, if local, success by this method. The German strategy and tactics of last year were but a logical development of the Great War methods, a development that corresponded to the improved quality of the machines available, to a better understanding of the tactics best suited to their employment and to a strategy which looked beyond the breakthrough of the hostile position to a war of movement.

Even during the last war the British protagonists of the tank, notably Mr Winston Churchill and Colonel Fuller, advocated their employment upon lines which were much more like the German methods of 1940 than were the British and French ideas. The latter clung closely to the methods of the last war and seem to have been completely blind to the lessons of the Battle of Cambrai and to the battle of 8 August 1918. About 1930 the British were proceeding with the development of large armoured units on the lines since adopted by the Germans but they did not proceed far and before the outbreak of the present war they seem to have reverted back to the tactics and strategy of the last war, i.e. to the close association of tanks with infantry and artillery and away from the idea of a mechanical cavalry. General de Gaulle's book, in which he advocated the ideas adopted by the Germans, has received much notice and it is even suggested that the Germans adopted his ideas! But the book of history was open to all soldiers and the manufacturers and inventors were only too eager to show the continuous improvement of their products. Colonel (later General) Fuller persistently advocated methods now vindicated in battle and became so exasperated at the impossibility of moving 'the machine' that his advocacy became uncomfortable to the authorities. He resigned when they proposed to put him away in India where his efforts at reform would not trouble them. As a further illustration of the fact that the German method of 1940 is not new, the writer may be forgiven for mentioning that he published eleven years ago an outline of the tactical method followed by the Germans and in so doing anticipated by some six years General de Gaulle (see *An t-Óglach*, July 1930).

In spite of the fact that the French were unable to meet this form of attack, nothing has publicly transpired about the campaigns of 1940 which should shake our confidence in our own theory of defence against it. If our means and our preparations are equal to our theory, we will stop it … The German tanks did two things.

They played their part with other means in punching a hole in the Allied line and they operated in conjunction with aircraft great distances behind the battlefield upon which the main forces were engaged. In this latter case they met little or no opposition because their enemies seem not to have realised in time the necessity for local defence measures all over their territories. Belts and areas of defended obstructions and adequate local guards and garrisons were not provided. These lightning advances would have led nowhere if the armoured units were not able to obtain supplies both in the territory invaded and by the rapid advance of supply elements from their rear.

Parachute Troops

The employment of parachute troops was new only in the sense that masses of them has not previously been employed in war. For several years these troops existed in Russia and Germany and much publicity was given to their largescale use in Russian manoeuvres. The Allies, however, do not seem to have thought out a reply to them. In this connection, it is of interest of recall that several years ago Mr Aiken, then Minister for Defence, asked our army authorities to produce an answer to this problem. The answer is now well known and, provided we are alert and determined and thorough, we need not fear the parachutes.

Sabotage

Sabotage of all kinds has not previously been employed so extensively and so successfully but it is in no sense a new method. It is merely a wide scale development of the methods employed by all intelligence service in the last war.

The infamous fifth columnists appear to have been more dangerous by reason of the moral effect and the confusion produced by them than because of the amount of actual material damage done. The sending of false orders, the spread of false information by fifth columnists, and also by enemy troops, had far-reaching effects in Norway, Holland and France. The first answer to this method of warfare is to attain that national unity, solidarity and discipline against which the saboteur, fifth columnist and propagandist are powerless. The second reply is to deal ruthlessly and with the speed of lightning with all traitors. Make it as unsafe an occupation as it was in the last year of the Anglo-Irish War and it will not flourish. The third reply is to guard and patrol vigilantly those places which saboteurs and fifth columnists are likely to attack or use. The fourth reply is to have our system of communication and of passing orders so watertight that it cannot be interfered with.

Infiltration Tactics

Those of our officers who attended command and staff courses at the Military College are familiar with these. The tactics of infiltration consist of probing the soft or weak spots of the enemy position and pushing on rapidly through these leaving the strong points to be surrounded and attacked by reserves coming from the rear. Those who describe them as new are not acquainted with the history of the Great War. These tactics were developed by the Germans in 1917 and applied with conspicuous success in the Battle of Cambrai and the March 1918 offensive ...

Lessons of History

The three battles of the last war to which reference has been made above have been studied by a great many of our officers. There are excellent histories of these battles and a mass of other literature dealing with them. They illustrate or point the way to almost all of the methods used by the Germans last year. If the lessons of these battles had been properly understood in France, M. Reynaud would not have said: 'Our classic conception of the conduct of war has come up against a new conception.'

NEW TYPE OF WARFARE?
PART II

by Colonel M.J. Costello

Other Reasons for German Success

It is no harm to repeat that the true and full account of the campaigns of 1940 is not available to anyone yet but there is sufficient information to indicate some of the methods employed by the Germans and some of the apparent reasons for their access. The reasons are to be found as much in the weakness of the defenders as in the methods and advantages of the attacker.

Those reasons which are apparent at the present time and which have not already been mentioned are:

1. Surprise
2. Morale
3. Leadership
4. Mobility
5. Endurance
6. Ruthlessness
7. Superior training
8. Employment of all possible means in co-operation
9. Superior numbers
10. Superior weapons

Surprise

Implicit in the statements of all of those who attribute the German victories to new methods is the admission that the most potent of all factors in battle, and one as old as man himself, was in favour of Germany. This factor is surprise. M. Reynaud's statement is eloquent on this matter. The plea for clear thinking in the hour of defeat is an admission that this essential was absent from the pre-war policy and plans of France. The superiority of the German air force and the superior mobility of the German armies were important factors in effecting these surprises but not more important than the ostrich-like attitude of the Allies. There are countless ways in which surprise may be achieved. There is only one general way of avoiding it, that is to prepare for every possible threat, no matter how remote it may seem, and then when all this is done, to be mentally prepared for the unexpected and to be always on the alert. The indispensable weapons of defence against surprise are keen active brains, always questioning, always examining, always trying to see into the future, always revising their plans – capable brains imbued with that 'divine discount' with things as they are. Since we are merely human, things will never be perfect for us, there will always be room for improvement.

We have the brains and we must use them. We must drive them with that restless energy which will brook no obstacle and which will regard every deficiency of material as a challenge to its ingenuity. Irish brains are as good as any in the world, and they should – every one of them – be actively employed to save our country.

Morale

There is not sufficient information available to discuss this factor at length but such information as there is indicates that the German forces were inspired by a moral fervour which was far more powerful

211

than that which animated the Allied armies. For years the mind of the German citizen and soldier had been impressed with the idea of the superiority of his race. The magnificent achievements of the old German army were held up for admiration and emulation. We have seen in our own country how the patriotic fervour of the pre-truce days inspired the IRA to deeds of daring endurance and martyrdom which would seem incredible to more cold-blooded generations and more matter-of-fact races. It was the religious fanaticism of the Cromwellians which gave them the discipline and morale that proved invincible. The revolutionary enthusiasm of the French armies of one hundred and fifty years ago more than compensated for their lack of training and equipment. It seems as if the spirit of the German army has been developed to a point at which it can be compared with these examples from the past. There was no such unity, cohesion and flaming spirit in France, and in England the fighting spirit has awakened slowly.

Leadership

The leadership of the German army has proved itself to be all that competent observers would expect of its training and selection. It has drive, skill and resolution. Its planning shows the utmost thoroughness. It neglected no means of obtaining an advantage. Of the subordinate leadership on the Allied side it is impossible to speak but the higher command, if judged by its action, lacked realism and lost its grip almost at the outset.

Mobility

In the superior mobility of the German armies there lay an advantage which in itself was overwhelming. No thoughtful soldier could have expected the immense masses of cavalry and horse transport of the Poles to be anything but helpless in the contest with the more compact, less vulnerable, and more mobile German columns. Although the Germans still use horses, the basis of their mobility is the motor vehicle. If the French or Polish division marched with its wagons fifteen miles in a day it did well. A motorised division would as easily do one hundred and fifty miles. The advantages of speed in movement are obvious enough to any intelligent mind and it was only pedantry and the weight of tradition which kept some armies on the transport basis of Bianconi's days while the civil life of the same countries used twentieth-century transportation. Even in more favourable circumstances it would have been quite impossible for the French to move their old-fashioned divisions with sufficient speed to counter the lightning German thrusts and to punish these unsupported bounds of the Panzer divisions. It was like matching fifteen hurlers with the speed of snails against the Limerick county team. One might as well expect a team of Clydesdale horses to race the motor cyclists of the 3rd Motor Squadron.

Endurance

The mobility of the German army was based on motors or even on foot it was more mobile because of the superior powers of endurance of its men. It is reported that units marched thirty miles in a day and fought at the end of the march. All history, as well as our common sense, shows us that this is a factor of great importance in battle. The capacity to withstand fatigue, hunger, cold and the ordeal of continuous fighting was highly developed. In a long day's battle the side which can stick it best and which can summon the greatest amount of energy at the end of the day is bound to win, other things being equal. From such information as is available, it appears that the power of endurance of none of the Allies was equal to that of the Germans.

Ruthlessness

As might be expected from the pre-war writings of Germans of influence and authority, the Germans appear to have been completely ruthless in waging war. They made straight for their object, the destruction of the enemy opposing them, and allowed nothing to stand in their way.

Training

From pre-war information it is clear that the German army was the best trained in Europe. Its pre-war training displayed a realism, thoroughness and earnestness which was not evident in any of the defeated armies. The British army was largely called into being after the German army had already been trained, and from such news as has appeared of its training in France, one must conclude that even then the time available was not used to the best advantage.

Co-operation

A feature of pre-war German training was the co-operation of all arms in battle. This intimate co-operation appears to have been realised in France and Belgium. It was especially important in the co-operation between aircraft and ground troops and between parachutists, fifth columnists and saboteurs and the advancing armies. It is a commonplace of football and hurling that team work is indispensable. How much more necessary it is in an army is apparent from a comparison of the variety and complexity of the army team with the uniformity of the fifteen men who make the hurling or football team. The Allies were not a team in this sense and even within each Allied army the cohesion and co-operation attained does not seem to have reached the German standard, Britain had not trained her army and air force to work intimately together.

Superior Numbers

The advantage in numbers was on the German side. During the decisive Battle of France that superiority was probably about two-to-one in ground forces. During the assaults on the Belgian and Dutch armies it was certainly much greater. Even more important was the decisive superiority of the German air force. In Holland this was overwhelming.

Superior Weapons

It appears that the German army was better equipped than its enemies. Up to the end of the last war there was a continuous increase in the proportion of automatic arms. Since the invention of fire-arms it has been plain that the fighting units of infantry should be able to shoot as many bullets per minute at the enemy as the development of weapons and means of transport would make possible without sacrificing mobility. This progressive increase in the volume of small arms fire of each infantry unit almost ceased in England and France when the world war ended. It continued in Germany so that the number of automatic arms at the disposal of her troops was much greater. For many years it has been a commonplace of progressive military thought that the rifle of the future is the automatic rifle. So far, only the USA and Finland have these. England and France fight with the rifle which they had at the beginning of the century and Germany's superiority in this matter rests only upon an increased number of light machine guns.

The German anti-aircraft guns are all designed for use against ground targets and the advantages of this arrangement whereby all kinds of light guns can engage tanks and almost all can engage aircraft have been apparent. Strange as it may seem, it took the actual trial of war to convince the great bulk of military opinion that the specialisation of these anti-aircraft, anti-tank and field guns was not the ideal policy. The French anti-tank gun was not sufficiently powerful and the war should not have been necessary to prove this. While the British weapons hit an adequate blow their absurd specialisation did not permit of them being available where they could have been most useful.

German anti-tank mines were more numerous and more powerful. The British and French mines were not as powerful as those used by the IRA at the end of the Anglo-Irish War.

German engineer equipment appears to have been excellent also but whether it was better than the British is not clear.

Not alone were the Allied means of anti-tank defence inadequate, but the Germans are said by some observers to have had superior tanks.

German Victory Inevitable

If the foregoing review is even approximately correct, it will be seen that there were sufficient factors in the German favour to make victory inevitable. In view of the uncertainty of the writer's information, he would ask the reader merely to count up those factors in which his own information or opinion gives the balance of advantage to Germany. It is likely that every informed reader will find a sufficient balance to explain the victories of last summer. In the accounts of the British victories in Libya many of the same factors will be seen in operation with similar results.

IRISH SOLDIERS ABROAD
THE STORY OF IRELAND'S EXILE SOLDIERS

by Colonel M.J. Costello, O/C, Southern Command

It is one of the paradoxes of our history that, while our country has produced some of the finest leaders and bravest soldiers in the world, their achievements have brought benefits to foreign countries rather than our own. The explanation of this lies in the centuries of oppression and dissension, which strangled our economic and political development up to 1916, and negatived all our efforts towards emancipation by force of arms.

And thus it is not surprising that our soldiers for three hundred years won their spurs chiefly on 'far, foreign fields'.

The foreign military achievements of our race began however, on our own account. We conquered and colonised Scotland, frequently invaded England during and after the Roman occupation of that country, and an Irish king died while leading his army at the foot of the Alps.

Soon the Norsemen gave us enough fighting at home. When these had been overthrown at Clontarf, only a century and a half elapsed until the invasion from England began. From the time of Elizabeth's plantation of Munster Irishmen again fought abroad but in the armies of foreign powers. After the Cromwellian settlement, the agents of the king of Spain, the king of Poland and the prince of Conde competed for the service of Irish troops. In May 1652, 7,000 went to Spain, and they were followed in September of the same year by 3,000 more. Lord Muskerry took 5,000 to serve the king of Poland. In three years, 34,000 left their native land according to Prendergast, the historian of the period.

After the Williamite wars, an even greater exodus took place. Then the penal laws, the confiscations and proscription at home kept up the stream of exiles. During the nineteenth-century famine and eviction sent hundreds of thousands to America who largely fought the wars of the new republic.

The Irish have always been a military people. War has been the ruling passion of our race. Everywhere they went Irish soldiers earned a reputation second to none. Dean Swift said 'he could not esteem too highly those gentlemen of Ireland who with all the disadvantages of being exiles and strangers have been able to distinguish themselves in so many parts of Europe by their valour and conduct above that of all other nations'. Even bitter enemies of our race, like Sir John Norris, and Spencer the poet, give unstinted praises to the soldierly qualities of the Irish. William of Orange who was in a good position to judge said they were born soldiers.

The story of Ireland's exiled soldiers is a long one. It would lead one through the history of almost every civilised country, and it would cover centuries of time. In the following paragraphs it will only be possible to mention representative facts and names so as to convey a general impression rather than a detailed account of the military achievements of our people.

Irish Soldiers of France

For centuries France was our friend, and it was naturally to her that the soldier of fortune offered his sword. The Irish were well received there. They were befriended by the court and welcomed by the army. A French military historian estimates that as many as 750,000 Irishmen died in the service of France between 1650 and 1800. McGeoghegan, the historian who was chaplain of the Irish Brigade, says that 450,000 served in the years from 1691 to 1745.

The first Irish Brigade in the service of France was composed of Irish units taken from Ireland in exchange for French units sent to this country to fight for James the Second. Well disciplined, well trained and well led, these units won renown on many a battlefield.

At Cremona in Italy, six hundred of them made such a determined and skilful resistance to a besieging Austrian army that in spite of surprise and greatly superior numbers, the Austrians, under the great Prince Eugene, were defeated in their attempt to capture the place. Prince Eugene said their defence was a miracle and Europe rang with their fame. They lost three hundred and fifty men on this day. Their commander, Major O'Mahony was personally received and warmly thanked by the king of France, and the pay of the men was raised in recognition of their services. At Fontenoy, the Irish Brigade, as part of the French reserves, made a famous charge which was the decisive factor in a decisive battle. It won the admiration of friend and foe; and was the inspiration of Thomas Davis' spirited poem.

Towards the end of the eighteenth century the number of recruits from Ireland began to fall off, and the history of this Irish Brigade ends at the time of the French Revolution – Louis XVIII conveyed the gratitude of France for their services when he presented a standard with these words: 'Gentlemen, we acknowledge the inappreciable services that France has received from the Irish Brigade in the last one hundred years; services we shall never forget, though under an impossibility of requiting them. Received this standard as a pledge of our remembrance, a monument of our admiration, and of our respect; and in future generous Irishmen, this shall be the motto of your spotless flag:

'1692–1792

ALWAYS AND EVERYWHERE FAITHFUL'

Thomas Davis was well justified in saying that 'when valour becomes a reproach, when patriotism is thought a prejudice and when a soldier's sword is a sign of shame the Irish Brigade will be despised or forgotten'.

Napoleon formed an Irish legion and this was the only one of his numerous foreign corps, which was entrusted with an Imperial Eagle. After the Napoleonic Wars a free America attracted our emigrants. Only the descendants of the Wild Geese continued to fight for France, and the descendants of corps which were decimated time and time again are naturally not numerous.

The Irish in France produced many leaders. General Kilmaine was born in Dublin. He was a friend and confidant of Napoleon whom he succeeded in the command of the army organised for the invasion of England. He died young but his services in the Revolutionary Wars mark him as one of the most brilliant soldiers of his time. General James O'Moran, born in the parish of Ross, Elphin diocese, fought in American and in the Revolutionary Wars. He was executed like many others during the rein of terror, but the gratitude and esteem of the French nation is expressed in the inscription of his name on the Arc de Triomphe in company with the greatest soldiers of France.

General Lally, whose family came from Tullaghnadaly, Tuam was another worthy representative of our race. The great Marshal Saxe observed during a critical period of French history: 'We can sleep peacefully for Lally is with the army'. He made a great effort to retain French influence and power in India. Even his English enemies acknowledge his merits. Descendants of the Wild Geese include General Louis Cavaignac, a French minister for war and Marshal Patrick MacMahon, a president of the French Republic.

Irish Soldiers of Spain

When the Spanish infantry was the finest in the world, Spain sought eagerly for Irish soldiers. From 1600 to the beginning of last century there were Irish units in the Spanish army. During the early part of the eighteenth century, there were hundreds of Irish officers as well as five Irish Regiments, those of Waterford, Limerick, Hibernia, Ultonia and Irelanda called 'The Famous'. The last three survived to fight Napoleon. These regiments were officered only by Irishmen.

Sir Charles Oman, in his *History of the Peninsular War*, writes: 'An astounding proportion of the officers who rose to some note during the war bore Irish names and were hereditary soldiers of fortune who justified their existence by the unwavering courage which they always showed ... Their constant readiness to fight, which no series of defeats could tame, contrasts very well with the spiritless behaviour of many of the Spanish generals. No officer of Irish blood was ever found among the cowards and hardly one among the traitors. The whole Spanish army was full of officers of Irish name and blood, the sons and grandsons of original emigrants'. To name but a few they were: Blake, two O'Donnells, Lacy, Sarsfield, O'Neill, O'Daly, Maloney and O'Donoghue. Blake was in real merit the outstanding soldier of the Spanish army in the Peninsular War. A great organiser, he was skilful, brave and determined, and stands in marked contrast to the average Spanish commander of the period. An O'Donnell became Duke of Tetuan and Field Marshal of Spain. Ambrose Higgins, of County Meath was the foremost Spanish soldier in Chile and Peru. James McKenna was Spain's greatest military engineer. A son of Ambrose O'Higgins was foremost among those who fought for and gained Chilean independence, and one of his chief lieutenants was Colonel Charles Patrick Madden, from Maryland, USA.

The pre-eminence of the Irish soldiers in Spain was as marked as that of the exiles in France. One instance of their great services was the defence of Gerona 1808. Three hundred and fifty men of the Irish Regiment of Ultonia and 2,000 Spanish civilians held the town against the most determined assaults of 6,000 French. Contemporary writers give the highest possible praise to the gallant Colonel Henry Donovan who commanded the Irish troops.

THE PRINCIPLES OF WAR

by Colonel M.J. Costello[*]

Nature of War

With war raging all round us, it is not necessary to describe at length its nature to those who read the newspapers. We see it as a conflict between peoples involving the whole nation at war and all its resources, mental, moral and physical. It is however necessary to remind soldiers that they should not become so absorbed in the details of their own preparations for defence as to ignore or forget the wider aspects of the vast conflict which war is. The military operations for which they prepare should be visualised against the background of a struggle in other spheres of activity. They should do this so as to be mentally prepared for any eventuality and so as to apply the military force at their command in harmony with the other aspects of the national struggle. War, as all can see, is a struggle in which each side uses every means in its power to impose its will upon the other. Besides land, sea and air forces, these means include:

(1) Propaganda, tending to break the will of the enemy, or at least to mislead him, or to weaken him in some way or another.

---

[*] This article and the three following are extracts from a much longer essay published in separate sections.

(2) Economic pressure, aiming at the starvation of the enemy and especially at the cutting off of commodities essential to the prosecution of war.

(3) Sabotage, which uses every device to impede and disrupt the preparation and execution of defensive measures and indeed the whole life of the state.

Defeat

Defeat is a moral result. A nation or an army is beaten, not when it has lost a certain proportion of its territory, or even its means of waging war but only when it has no longer got the will to resist. The enemy's will to win is therefore the general object of attack in war and the maintenance of the resolution of our own people is of paramount importance. Defeat – the collapse of the national will – may be brought about by terror, discouragement, a belief that the object of the war is no longer attainable, or that its attainment is not worth the cost.

Military Operations: factors that decide the issue

While military forces are but one of the means of waging war, they are the nation's principal shield against attack and they are the spearhead of its attack upon the enemy. Their victories will immensely strengthen the national will and provide material for attacking the morale of the enemy through propaganda. Their bearing in defeat will profoundly influence the attitude of the people to reverses.

Victory or defeat in battle is very largely a moral result also. As Foch has said 'a battle lost is one we believe to be lost', but of course many things operate in creating the belief. The factors that decide the issue of a battle may be said to be these:

Moral Factors

    (a) Morale (the fighting spirit)

    (b) Discipline

Skill and Training

    (b) Skill of the leaders

    (c) Skill of the men

    (d) Powers of endurance

    (e) Organisation

Material Factors

    (a) Armament

    (b) Numbers

    (c) Supply

    (d) Ground

Moral Factors

Since defeat is a moral result, the moral factors are of first importance. These will be dealt with separately (see page 246).

Relative Skill

The skill of the leaders is shown in the manner in which they develop all other factors to their own advantage and to the disadvantage of the enemy.

The skill of every individual man counts in the modern battle. His intelligence and initiative must be developed to the fullest extent if he is to apply his skill to the best advantage. The day of the soldier who acted like a cog in a machine, who merely executed automatically the orders given to him, is long past. It is merely necessary to compare the solid squares and regular shoulder-to-shoulder lines of the past with the distribution of a modern platoon in attack or defence, or with an ambush party, to see that a mechanical man will win no battle nowadays. The private soldiers, besides being intelligent and skilful in the use of his weapons and of the ground, must thoroughly understand what the object of his platoon or section is in each operation. He must have as clear an idea of the objective of his company as the company commander of a hundred years ago found necessary. His own survival and the success of his unit depend upon his using his head and upon his being as intelligent and understanding a member of his military team as the individual footballer is who knows every move of the game and whose team work is based upon this understanding.

The strain of battle is terrific. Only the highest quality of morale and discipline will enable a man to stand the mental strain. But the physical strain is just as great. The value of any man or any unit depends directly upon the amount of work that he or it can put into the winning of victory. The side which can march fastest and farthest and endure most hardship has a very great advantage. In every war this advantage has been marked. Instead of being less important now in this age of machinery, it becomes even more important on account of the swiftness of operations. The Germans understood this well in the last war when they developed especially the powers of endurance of the shock troops who shattered the British front in France in 1918. Their campaigns in 1940 show that they are still alive to its importance.

The side with the best organisation has an obvious advantage. The aims of organisation are to fit each man, weapon and tool into its place in the complete machine, to place each where it can produce the best results, to provide in advance for every need, to secure the smooth, rapid and efficient response of the whole force to orders from the top and at the same time to secure that flexibility and adaptability which is essential to meet a changing situation.

Material Factors

These need no elaboration. Better weapons, greater numbers, better supplies, all confer advantages which the stronger in them should exploit and which the weaker will attempt to neutralise. They are the factors in battle which are most tangible and most easily assessed. The other material factor – the ground – including the fortifications and other artificial features of it, is also of obvious importance. The art of tactics consists to a great extent of using it with skill.

The Scientific Side of War

The foregoing factors can also be classified from another point of view, namely, into those material factors which can be dealt with in an exact manner, such as organisation, ground, armament, etc., and into those human factors which cannot be dealt with as an exact science. Such are the moral factors and the skill of the combatants. The material factors change with every development of civilisation, with each new device which can be used in the struggle and the soldier must study the world about him, examine the means of waging peace so as to exploit all of them in the struggle for existence which is war. The alert, active mind which seized on the idea of applying to war the caterpillar track, developed to meet the needs of the American farmer and lumberman produced the tank, a weapon which might have won the last war for the Allies in 1917 if the skill and judgment of their soldiers had been equal to the opportunity. The means of fighting which industry and science make available have seldom been exploited as soon and as thoroughly as they might be. The organisation of the national resources and of the military forces have seldom been so thorough as they could be and these delays and neglects have been paid for in blood and tears and treasure. All this, which may be termed the scientific side of war, requires to be directed with an understanding of the nature of war, and its fruits can be applied successfully in battle only by those who understand thoroughly the other – the human – factors.

The Art of War

In the conduct of a campaign or of a battle we are concerned with the arts of strategy and tactics. Strategy deals with the employment on a broad scale of our means of waging war up to the commencement of each individual battle. Where strategy ends, tactics begin. Strategy is the province of the general, tactics begin. Strategy is the province of the general, tactics the province of the subordinate leader. Here we deal with the practical application of knowledge and natural ability in order to defeat the enemy, with the skilful employment of all means available to attain this end. We can call this the art of war which uses and applies the products of the scientific side of war but which deals mainly with the human factors.

Since man is the most constant, as he is the most important factor in battle, we have all the experience of the past to guide us to an understanding of what I have termed the human factors. Relatively speaking, these factors have hardly changed since the dawn of history. From the study of history, we see that certain experiences are repeated over and over again. We see that the great leaders of the past, while they were all original in some way or another, had certain methods in common. We see that the neglect of similar matters has led to disaster time and time again. We see that he who surprised his enemy thereby gained a great advantage, that superior mobility was a great advantage, and that the leader who carefully chose his goal or object and used all his efforts to attain it had the better of the one who was distracted from his object, who tried to do several things at once, who changed from one objective to another before he had attained the first. We see that a force that acts together, each for all and all for each, is much more powerful than the same force with its several units acting independently.

These and other experiences recurring again and again in the history of war enable us to make generalisations for our future guidance. These generalisations, established from experience, we call principles.

It is important to note the distinction between a principle and a rule. There are no rules of tactics like there are rules of discipline. It is a principle that a commander should provide for the security of his force. It is a rule that the commander's sentries should not sleep at their posts. If we think of them as methods by which certain results have generally been obtained, it will be the best way of remembering the use of these principles in action.

The Principles of War

The generalisations or principles that we deduce from history are these:

- The Objective
- Surprise
- Security
- Economy of Force

- Co-operation
- Mobility
- The Offensive
- Concentration
- Mass
- Simplicity

There is nothing mysterious in these methods or principles. They are simply what our common sense would tell us to do or to avoid if our common sense were enlightened by enough knowledge of war. They are the common sense of all past experience in tactics and strategy – common sense guides to action.

But in order to understand them fully, we should study the historical events which illustrate them. In this illustration of the principles of war lies one of the main advantages of historical study.

THE PRINCIPLES OF WAR
PART II – THE OBJECTIVE

by Colonel M.J. Costello

The ultimate objective in war is a better peace and this can be attained by overcoming the enemy's will. There will be a large number of subsidiary objective each leading up to the ultimate objective. There should be one principal objective at a time. If there is a subsidiary one, it should be such as to help directly in securing the main end. The choice of the objective from time to time is one of the most important functions of the leader of the force engaged. It should be an objective which is suitable to our military power and other things being equal most damaging to the enemy. Every military plan and each aspect of a plan should be tested by its bearing upon the attainment of the objective. We should ask ourselves what is the object, what is the most effective way of attaining it, and of every plan ask does it lead us to our objective? While continuous activity is essential in war, it is equally necessary that this activity should not be aimless.

It will be noticed how the Germans have during the present war concentrated all their efforts upon the attainment of one object a time. In the story of Crossbarry can be seen how the commander's plan was based upon a clear-cut objective and when this was attained he carefully avoided further conflict for the day. In even the smallest fight we must be clear as to our aim and if the objective is not indicated to us we must choose it with care and stick to it.

In order that we may be in position to choose the best objective, we must have the fullest possible information about the enemy. There must be a continuous effort by all ranks to help in building up the stock of information which when pieced together enables us to picture the enemy's situation and choose the most profitable object of attack.

In everyday life this principle is well understood. It is enshrined in the saying, 'The world turns aside to let pass the man who knows where he is going.'

Napoleon's brilliant successes in war were to a great extent due to the fact that his mind was fixed upon his final objective – the destruction of the enemy, while his early enemies and indeed all military leaders of the generation before his, wasted their power upon meaningless manoeuvres or upon objectives which were not decisive or were not worth the cost of attaining them. Napoleon's only violation of this principle cost him dear. He took an expeditionary force to Egypt with the object of embarking upon a great scheme of conquest in the east. While his land forces were superb his means did not justify the adoption of this objective since England controlling the seas could and did cut him off from France and made it impossible for him to maintain his army.

In the early stages of his invasion of Russia Napoleon kept after his true objective, the Russian armies, but he later became obsessed with the idea of taking Moscow and it, rather than the enemy, became his objective. It was only when he had taken Moscow that he realised that he had followed a will o' the wisp and that the capture and destruction of its capital would not break the will of a determined nation.

During the last Great War the British sent an expedition to the Dardanelles which ended in complete failure. One of the principal reasons for the failure was the fact that the object was not clearly defined at the outset and the means employed were not properly related to the task. In fact, Britain drifted into the campaign and paid for her drifting.

In the Battle of Cambrai is also seen how the violation of these principles of war is punished. The confusion about the objective of the battle and the failure to relate the means to the object ultimately sought made the British failure almost inevitable. What could have been an outstanding successful raid became, in fact, a muddle.

The greater German victory of the last war in France – that of March, 1918 – was not a decisive victory because no objective vital to the Allies was taken and the defeat of the British Fifth Army did not lead to any further advantage.

THE PRINCIPLES OF WAR
PART III – SURPRISE

by Colonel M.J. Costello

It is easy to understand the importance of this principle. It has always been the most effective method of securing victory. History teems with examples of its effect and each one of us will have experienced in everyday life the paralysing and disorganising effect of a sudden shock.

Readers of the historical articles in this paper will have noted that in each of the fights which have been described surprise was a factor essential to success. During the 1914–1918 war, every German offensive in France which achieved surprise was successful in its early stages at any rate. The first of the series of great offensives in 1918 which failed utterly was the one for which the Allies were prepared – the one that did not achieve surprise.

It is unnecessary to detail the effect of surprise in the present war since it will be plain even from the newspaper reports.

The methods by which surprise may be achieved are countless. Every keen soldier should continuously seek out new ways of securing the enormous advantage which surprise in battle gives. We should, by a careful study of history and of the world around us, ensure that we are not surprised by old methods or by the application to war of some weapon, device or method already used for peaceful purposes but not previously applied to war.

Some of the methods which have been used to secure surprise are:

- Secrecy in plans and preparations
- Misleading the enemy
- Daring to do what is thought impossible and, therefore, unexpected by the enemy
- Use of new methods of any kind
- Use of new weapons or equipment
- Unexpected speed

Secrecy

If the enemy can get a inkling of our plans it is obvious that we cannot surprise him. The less he knows about us the more difficult it will be for him to predict or calculate what we are about or even what it is possible for us to do. Even seemingly unimportant items of information are helpful to him in so far as they help him to an understanding our powers and characteristics. This is why we have to insist that the army and LDF will not talk before strangers about military matters and they will disclose no military information however trivial to any person whose duties do not require him to have it. We rely upon every citizen as well as every member of the armed forces to stop every leakage of information by reporting promptly every instance which he or she notices. Night movements often resorted to in the past in order to preserve secrecy are more necessary than ever since the development of the aeroplane. The importance of all training in night operations cannot be overemphasised.

Careful consideration and good judgement are required in

deciding how much information about plans may be given to subordinates. The more fully they are informed the more intelligent and thorough their co-operation is likely to be but the more widely information of a secret nature is distributed the greater the danger of a loss or leakage.

Misleading the Enemy

Stonewall Jackson gave it as his prescription for victory that we should mystify, mislead and surprise the enemy, and his advice is borne out by all the experience of the past. By secrecy we can mystify the enemy but it is also desirable to take positive steps to mislead him in every possible way. The most notable of all writers on war – Von Clausewitz – said that a talent for artifice and stratagem was one of the chief characteristics of good leadership.

A competent intelligence service will find means of supplying the enemy with misleading information and it will be effectively prevented from doing this by one thing only and that is amateur efforts by people on its own side. If a plausible but misleading story is conveyed to the enemy by our intelligence, the effect may be lost if someone else on our side puts out a different story in the hope of misleading him. There is need for the effort of everyone in preventing the enemy from getting information about us, but the uninitiated will do more harm than good if they butt in on the delicate task of the expert who is 'putting across' a story which the enemy may be got to believe.

The use of dummy guns, dummy mines, dummy entrenchments and other positions can be practised by even the smallest military units. The skilful use of motor transport makes many deceptions possible. An empty bus or covered lorry looks the same from the air as a full one. Tracks that lead nowhere are no different from tracks that lead somewhere. Since an extra ten or twenty miles make very little difference in a troop movement by motor transport the apparent destination of the movement can be a false one, or the front of advance can be so wide that the point of concentration will not be apparent until the last moment.

During the last war, the British army in Palestine completely overwhelmed the Turks in a battle which began on 18 September 1918. The British plans were brilliantly prepared and an important feature of them was the elaborate care taken to mislead the enemy. The British made their main attack on their left along the Mediterranean coast, but they succeeded in leading the Turks to expect the attack on the other flank – miles away. How this was done by the British commander Allenby is described by one of his staff officers who is now General Wavell and the British commander in chief in the Middle East:

He kept his cavalry on his right in the Jordan Valley to the last possible moment, and then moved two cavalry and one infantry division and many other units by night from the Jordan valley to the Judean hills on the coast. The camps of the troops already on the coast had some time previously been spread out. For instance, the battalions in reserve had each occupied with half a battalion a camp which would hold a whole battalion. As the troops came in from the right, each of these camps was filled by a whole battalion, so that no change was visible from the air. The camps in the Jordan valley were left standing, additional camps were added, and during the day-time mules were kept busy dragging bundles of bushwood to raise dust, and to make observation difficult and give an appearance of activity. Fifteen thousand dummy horses filled with straw occupied the deserted horse lines, and battalions from Jerusalem were marched down in daylight to the Jordan on several days in succession and brought back in lorries by night. Elaborate and very public preparations were made for transferring GHQ to Jerusalem, where an hotel was taken over, from which officers on leave were turned out, much to their indignation, and from which ran a full equipment of telegraph and telephone lines. Lastly, on the eve of the battle our Arab allies under the direction of Lawrence attacked the railway about Deraa Junction behind the Turkish left, and the junction was simultaneously bombed heavily by air force. After these artifices, combined with the superiority which our airmen attained, enabled the concentration on the coast to be completed without any indication of it reaching the enemy, and the battle was practically won before a shot was fired.

Even when it is not possible completely do deceive the enemy about our preparations it may be possible to keep him on the horns of a dilemma by preparing for two or more separate operations so that he will not know until the battle opens which is the real threat. The great mobility of motor transport makes this method more feasible than in the past.

Surprise by Daring

A careful, alert and thorough enemy will leave nothing to chance but opportunities for surprise may occur if he depends for his security on the belief that a course of action is too difficult for us to be attempted. There are many historical examples of surprise being achieved by daring to do the seemingly impossible. It is no exaggeration to say that England won Canada through the daring of Woulf who surprised and thereby defeated the French when he climbed the heights of Abraham by a path which the French believed to be impracticable and left unguarded.

Napoleon gained an immense advantage in 1800 when he descended on Italy in such a way as to surprise completely his Austrian enemies. By astounding efforts he brought his army over the Alps, a feat which the Austrians believed impossible and for which they were entirely unprepared.

Surprise by New Methods

Napoleon's whole strategy and tactics were so novel that with his inspired leadership he had little difficulty in overwhelming vastly superior forces of troops better equipped and even more thoroughly trained. The novelty of his methods so completely unbalanced and paralysed his earlier opponents that they are said to have remarked that it was 'impossible to fight this young man – he knew none of the rules of warfare'.

Every great leader in history has been distinguished for his originality and has made use of it to surprise his enemy.

During the last world war the Germans won an initial success at Verdun by a new method of employing their artillery. They again surprised their enemies when they developed methods of opening an artillery bombardment without previous registration. At Riga, and at Cambrai in 1917 and even four months later in March 1918, offensive they reaped great advantages from the employment of a new method of attack, the now well-known method of infiltration.

When they developed new methods of defence to correspond to the new tactics of attack they achieved surprise with these also.

During the present war surprises have been achieved by methods for which the Allies seem to have been unprepared and were, therefore, new to their official doctrine even though they were well known to many soldiers.

Surprise by New Weapons

The use by the Germans of heavy mobile howitzers surprised the

Allies in 1914. The use of gas surprised them in 1915 but in this case the Germans themselves were surprised at its success and did not reap the benefit of it. Although the British used tanks long before Cambrai and thus disclosed their secret to the Germans, the latter did not realise the potentialities of the new weapon and were thoroughly surprised by them at Cambrai.

Unexpected Speed

Unexpected speed of movement has on countless occasions secured surprise.

THE PRINCIPLES OF WAR
PART IV – SECURITY

by Colonel M.J. Costello

The principle of security is the corollary of the principle of surprise. While we should strain every nerve to surprise the enemy, we should neglect no means of securing ourselves against surprise. But the principle of security tells us also to take every possible step, such as concealment, fortification, good tactical disposition, which will tend to protect us against enemy action. It might be called the principle of preparedness. Security ensures freedom of action. It allows troops to move or rest undisturbed, and this is its main object.

One of the maxims of Frederick the Great is that it is pardonable to be defeated but never to be surprised. 'If the enemy is closely watched,' say British field service regulations, 'surprise will be impossible.'

Napoleon said that every plan of campaign must be based upon a sound and well-considered security – 'I endeavour to conjure up all possible dangers, to foresee all difficulties' – and he says: 'Military science consists in weighing carefully all possible eventualities and then eliminating, almost mathematically, chance. It is here that no error must be made, for a decimal more or less may change everything.'

Foch says in his *Principles of War*: 'We must constantly penetrate our minds with this necessity of safeguarding, above all, our own freedom of action, if we want to find ourselves, at the end of an operation free, that is, victorious. A constant preoccupation, while we prepare and combine an action against the enemy, must be to escape his will, to parry any undertaking by which he might prevent our action from succeeding. Any military idea, any scheme, any plan must therefore be connected with the conception of security. We must, as if we were fencing, attack without uncovering ourselves, parry without ceasing to threaten the adversary.'

Throughout history, we find that those who were boldest and most successful in action were the most cautious and thorough in the preparation of their first plans. In an earlier article, I have drawn attention to the security measures taken at Crossbarry. The West Cork column was as daring a unit as any of which we have record, but this absolute fearlessness did not lead to carelessness or disregard for security measures.

In these days of aircraft, submarines, fast-moving tanks and concentration on sabotage, all parts of a state are liable to attack and security measures must embrace the whole national territory and all its vital interests.

Sentries, guards, outposts, advanced flank and rearguards, and protected road blocks, are all provided for security purposes, but the most valuable security measure of all is to keep such a close and constant watch upon the enemy that he is unable to move or act unknown to us. The importance of having every single person co-operate with our intelligence service is clear in this connection.

Security does not justify timidity. 'Caution in planning, boldness in execution, are the key to security', says General Maurice in *British Strategy* and he goes on to say, 'In planning, conjure up, as Napoleon advised, every possible difficulty and danger, but, having provided for these as far as human forethought can do so, never take counsel of your fears in action. In war our own difficulties and dangers always loom large and we are apt to forget those of the enemy, which are probably as great if not greater. Boldness in execution involves taking risks, and the responsible commander must be sole judge of when risks taken in the execution of his plan are justifiable. The calculation of risks involves a nice consideration of the factors of time and space. An army whose flanks or communications are threatened before it can endanger the flanks and communications of the enemy is obliged to conform. "Thrice armed is he who gets his blow in first", and therefore swift and resolute action is a far better means of providing security than the attempt to be safe everywhere, which usually means being safe nowhere.'

I have said that boldness in action is usually the best course, given that the means are available. Means are not confined to numbers. They include superior mobility, superior generalship, and more favourable conditions of time and space.

The historical incidents already mentioned as illustrating the principle of surprise also illustrate the necessity for security. Despite Frederick's maxim, which seems but elementary common sense, there are many instances in war of troops having been surprised and lost by the neglect of security measures. During the present war, the security of lines of communications and vital points in the interior seems to have been neglected in many cases.

In *Historical Illustrations to Field Service Regulations*, Eady quotes the following account of a French eyewitnesses of the Franco Prussian War of 1870:

> From that moment (midday, August 8) until we reached Lunev-ille, their scouts watched us unceasingly. Linked to their army by horsemen, they gave an exact account of our positions, our halts, our movements, and as they watched us from some little distance, incessantly appearing and disappearing, they spread uneasiness. In place of acting in a similar manner, we kept our cavalry in masses, difficult to move, which did not protect the army, and rendered no service whatsoever.
>
> For one moment, the Prussian staff lost our tracks in the

plains of Champagne, because we suddenly changed our plans. But they quickly found us again by means of their cavalry, which never lost touch and marched on our flanks, spreading out a curtain behind which their army worked. When he arrived at Chene Popule, the enemy was thirty miles behind his cavalry; as we advanced, we met groups of five or six horsemen who retired slowly, after examining our arrangements and informing those who followed them. If we wished to pursue, each fraction fell back on a support capable of resisting us and keeping us from penetrating the curtain. This service was so well performed by the Prussian cavalry that we marched, so to speak, within a net which enclosed us in its meshes.

SOME COMMENTS ON THE PRINCIPLES OF WAR

by Professor James Hogan, D. Litt,
University College Cork

Napoleon would have included, I imagine, speed or economy of time among the principles of war. Did he not say during the Italian campaign: 'I may lose battles, but I will never lose time'?

There is finally the unknown factor, which is sometimes a function of the morale of an army as a whole, but more often a function of the genius of the commander; but which has time and again proved to be the decisive element in battle. To this I think Colonel Costello does not refer in his article on 'The Principles of War'. The inspiration which caused Marlborough at Blenheim suddenly to change his order of battle, to gather his squadrons in a new line, and send them against the French centre, with infantry supports, is a good example of the unknown factor which the inspired commander introduces into battle. Had Napoleon done the same at Waterloo, the might have been his. Were it not for this unpredictable factor war might be regarded as a science, instead of being regarded as an art, as it is.

I offer these criticisms with the greatest diffidence since my acquaintance, as a historian, with war is with the science of making war which is not to be confused with the art of war. The latter is the soldier's business; the science of making war on the other hand is that of the politician and the publicist, and it is a much less respectable business; the historian engages retrospectively in the latter business.

The Moral Factor

To return to the moral factor. The task of war, as of revolution, consists in breaking the will of the enemy, forcing him to surrender and accept the conditions of the conqueror. The will is of course a fact of the psychical world. War seeks to dominate the psychical world – the will of the individual, the army, the nation – by physical force. Therefore war seeks to obtain a definite result, namely the disintegration of the will of the enemy, by applying force not directly on the mental and moral level of the will but indirectly on the physical level. Pressure on the physical plane, may, if sufficient, react on the psychical plane and there produce the desired state of mind; but this possibility of dominating the psychical world by the application of physical or material force arises from the fact that human personality constitutes a unity. Nevertheless it is true that the will, being a psychic fact, does evade direct contact with the physical world. There are therefore almost no limits to the resistance which the will is capable of offering to physical no less than to mental pressure. Broadly speaking, the amount of physical force necessary to overcome the will of the enemy will be in proportion to the enemy's will to maintain itself actively in war and by passive resistance if defeated. Strictly speaking, since there is no limit to the potentiality of the will to resist, the will of an army or of an nation to conquest is also limitless. But in practice the capacity of individuals to resist varies so much that a people or a nation or an army will, generally speaking yield morally as well as physically to overwhelming physical force. There may be of course individuals whose will to resist remains unbroken. The fact that the will on which the issue of battles, as the fate of nations, depends, belongs to the psychical world, introduces into battle and into the struggles between nations an unknown factor; the outcome is unpredictable. Superiority of material and numbers on one side may be neutralised by superiority of morale on the other. The campaigns of Frederick the Great, Montrose, Cromwell, Napoleon, Kosciusko, all demonstrate the enormous importance of the moral factor.

I was interested to note that despite what has been said about the elimination of man by the machine, it is stressed in the article that actually increasing mechanisation of the material means of war has so far from diminishing, enhanced the importance of the moral and human factor. It should be obvious that total war which involves all the levels of existence – intellectual, moral and material – thereby raises the moral and intellectual factors to a much higher potential as compared with the material factors than ever before.

Now that war has developed into a struggle between the wills of whole peoples the role of the armed forces retains its former military importance, while acquiring a new importance from the psychological point of view. It is the function of the army not only to shield the people from the material force of the enemy but also to leaven the mass of the people by acquiring and communicating by force of example the highest standards of devotion to duty and readiness for self-sacrifice.

The Soldier and the Martyr

The spirit of the perfect soldier and of the martyr have not a little in common. A martyr is primarily a soldier who takes it upon himself to bear witness to the supreme value and the absolute obligation of the military virtues in a situation in which his only means of giving his testimony is to sacrifice his own life on a forlorn hope. His self-sacrifice may have the aim of carrying his comrades to victory by breaking a breach in the enemy line, as when the Swiss soldier Arnold von Winkelried threw himself upon the Hapsburg pikes; or when the Italian Alessandro Pizzoli drew the fire of the enemy's cannon by dropping into the lane which the cannon commanded, and then charging the cannon's mouth at point-blank range; or when Sergeant Custume and his men rushed to certain death on the Bridge of Athlone. One of the most striking examples in history of the spirit which has inspired innumerable heroes who have died rather than surrender to an already victorious adversary, is illustrated by the famous story of two Spartan soldiers. The story relates that two men were in hospital together behind the front – both of them unfit for active service owing to an acute attack of ophthalmia – when the news reached them that the rest of their three hundred companions were being outflanked at Thermopylae by a turning movement and were therefore now doomed to certain death in consequence of the Spartan King Leonidas' decision not to retreat before the Persians. In these circumstances they both had the alternative of returning safely home to Sparta unless they preferred to lose their lives with their comrades, and, when this choice was presented to them, they could not make up their minds to agree, but took different views of their duty. While one slunk off home to Sparta, the other made his batman lead him to the battlefield; and when, upon reaching the front, the batman turned and fled, his master flung himself blind-eyed into the fight in order to meet death still more swiftly, and against still more fearful odds, than his two hundred and ninety-eight comrades whom he had rejoined – unbidden – by this heroic act of devotion. Here we have morale at its very highest, where in fact the attitude of the soldier is indistinguishable from that of the martyr. It may not be possible to create an army of the mettle of the three hundred who died to the last man at Thermopylae. But it is possible to develop in an army the military virtues to such a degree that even defeat leaves their will to self-sacrifice and ultimate victory unimpaired.

It must not be thought that the military virtues are in a class apart; they are virtues which are virtues in every walk of life, but strengthened and hardened by the sense of comradeship, duty and discipline. Courage, which is the most prominent of them, is a cardinal virtue in every action to which every human being can set his hand.

At an earlier stage in my argument, I accepted the thesis that the human will is by its nature capable of infinite resistance, and therefore is capable of excluding the state of mind associated with defeat. But this generalisation must be always qualified by the consideration that only exceptional individuals or groups exhibit this super-human will to victory. There are definite limits – though they should be set very high – to what may be achieved in the way of raising the morale of an army or a nation. When an individual or a government or a community mistakes the limits of the field of the military power, within which military power can be used with effect, or misconceives the nature of the objectives which it is possible to attain by its use, the practical consequences are likely to be fatal.

The action of challenge and response in the genesis of societies and civilisations is one of the best attested laws of history. In the absence of a challenge there is no response, no stimulus, and society stagnates; it loses the nerve to take the leap in the dark which marks all the forward movements of society. The question then arises whether we should accept the formula: 'The greater the challenge the greater the stimulus'. If we increase indefinitely the severity of the challenge to the life of a nation, a civilisation, a society, do we thereby ensure an indefinite intensification of the stimulus and, by this means, an indefinite increase of energy in the response which the challenge evokes? Or do we reach a point beyond which an increase in severity brings in diminishing returns? And if we go beyond this point, do we reach a further point at which the challenge becomes so severe that the possibility of responding to it successfully is eliminated altogether. The answer of history to this question is that when the severity of the challenge, whether it comes from human or material forces or from both, goes beyond a degree of severity, which I need not attempt do define here, the challenge becomes excessive, and the law of diminishing returns comes into operation. In other words, we have to recognize that however inexhaustible the resources of will may be, some challenges may be excessive; and it is the duty of the leaders of a nation to recognise when this limitation to what may be accomplished by sacrifice and valour exists.

Precisely the same considerations apply in the case of army; the commander must know how to distinguish between what is possible and impossible. While it is therefore true to say that 'defeat is a moral result', it is none the less true than the defeat of an army or nation, at least temporarily, may not be avoided by moral resources.

INDEX

Also available from Mercier Press

Rebel Ireland: From Easter Rising to Civil War

Sean McMahon

978 1 85635 498 1

This book brings together the three key events from which the Republic of Ireland evolved – the Easter Rising of 1916, the War of Independence of 1921 and the Civil War of 1922.

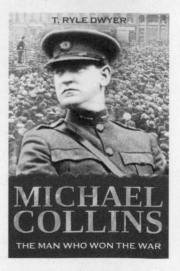

Michael Collins: The Man Who Won the War

T. Ryle Dwyer

978 1 85635 625 1

In this fully revised and updated analysis of Michael Collins' role in the War of Independence, T. Ryle Dwyer depicts Collins as both saint and sinner.